Praise for Bill Halamandaris' *The Heart of America*

"The Heart of America Foundation is making a wonderful difference! . . . By giving children an opportunity to be leaders and givers, you reveal the compassion and community spirit that truly is the heart of America."

Laura Bush
First Lady of the United States

"By personalizing the ten core values with moving stories of Americans both known and obscure, Bill Halamandaris provides a very human face for the ideas he presents. *The Heart of America* instructs readers as it moves them, and inspires as it educates."

Marcia Bullard
President & CEO, *USA WEEKEND* Magazine

"As this book demonstrates, the greatness of America is a reflection of the greatness of our people. There is something each of us can do to make the world a better place."

Christopher Reeve

"[Bill Halamandaris] remains one of the greatest inspirations that I have encountered in my life."

Robert Macauley
Founder, AmeriCares

"As the son of Italian immigrants, this book speaks to the values that gave them and millions like them the opportunity to live the American dream."

Leon Panetta
Chief of Staff, Clinton Administration

"I consider the work of the Heart of America Foundation to be very important. I send you my prayers and best wishes for the success of your humanitarian endeavor."

The Dalai Lama

"The history of our country has been each generation working and sacrificing to leave a better country to their children. As you read this book, ask yourself *what you can do to pass on a stronger, better country to future generations* . . . At this critical time, this must be our highest priority."

Ross Perot

"Bill Halamandaris makes it clear that the values that make America great—including generosity, selflessness, idealism, courage—are not the exclusive property of either side of the political spectrum. They are beyond politics—and for all of us to share and embody. This book will touch your heart and inspire your soul."

Arianna Huffington
Author of *Fanatics* and *Fools: The Game Plan*
for Winning Back America

"Bill Halamandaris, a man of great compassion himself, poignantly reminds us by numerous real life stories of just how fortunate we are to be American. *The Heart of America* should be required reading in every Civics class in America and in every high school graduating class in America."

Lloyd L. Hill
Chairman & CEO, Applebee's International

"I commend The Heart of America Foundation for giving young people the opportunity to learn that it is better to give than to receive and that in giving and receiving there is a profound joy that enriches the world."

Archbishop Desmond M. Tutu
recipient of the 1984 Nobel Peace Prize

"Bill Halamandaris and these inspiring stories puts us back in touch with the foundation of who we are as Americans. It is a first step on the path to finding our way again, to being the hope so many once aspired to be like. It is perfectly timed and much needed for all Americans."

Tim Love
Vice Chairman International, Saatchi & Saatchi

"The Heart of America Foundation does superb work."

Frances D. Fergusson
President, Vassar College

"A deeply moving collection of stories about people whose passions and commitments exemplify the goodness within the heart of America . . . a must read."

Don Perlyn
President, Miami Subs, Inc.

"Bill Halamandaris' book fully brings into focus the human spirit. It is simple and beautiful and brings forth personal courage, faith and love. This book has revealed a great truth—there is goodness in our world—you just have to open your heart."

Julia Kivistic
Vice President, Thompson and Murray

"Your work toward the betterment of mankind inspires us all."

Admiral Alan Shepard

"The Heart of America is doing such an enormously greatly needed job and truly making a difference! If you can produce a few more Bill Halamandaris' you will be a roaring success!"

Barbara Bush
Former First Lady of the United States

THE HEART OF AMERICA

Ten Core Values That Make Our Country Great

BILL HALAMANDARIS

Health Communications, Inc.
Deerfield Beach, Florida

www.bcibooks.com

Library of Congress Cataloging-in-Publication Data

Halamandaris, W., 1945–
    The heart of America : ten core values that make our country great / Bill
Halamandaris.
        p.   cm.
    Includes bibliographical references.
    ISBN 0-7573-0222-X (tp)
        1. Social values—United States.   2. Social ethics—United States.
    3. United States—Moral conditions.   4. National characteristics,
    American.   I. Title.

HN90.M6H33 2004
170'.973—dc22

2004047455

Publisher: Health Communications, Inc.
            3201 S.W. 15th Street
            Deerfield Beach, FL 33442-8190

Cover design by Larissa Hise Henoch
Inside book design by Dawn Von Strolley Grove

To be a good American means to understand the simple principles on which our nation was founded, to observe them in our daily life and to fight for them.

—Newbold Morris

For the people at the heart of America—
the Heart of America Foundation® family
and their kindred spirits—
all those who make America great.

Contents

Acknowledgments

Thanks must go to Bret Witter and Peter Vegso at Health Communications, Inc.: Bret for his vision in seeing the possibilities of this book and Peter for believing in it.

Thanks also to Bob Silverstein, my agent, for believing in me. I treasure our relationship.

Finally, I am indebted to all of those at the Heart of America Foundation® who supported this effort and facilitated the completion of this manuscript: particularly my wife Angela Halamandaris, Colleen Noland, Allison Pond and Susan Grimes.

Introduction

I have seen the best and worst of America. I have lived the American Dream and grown up with a deep appreciation for the gift it is to be an American.

My grandparents were among the 30 million people who emigrated to the United States during the first quarter of the last century. My father was a coal miner with a sixth-grade education.

When I was thirteen, Father told me he was dying. He said he had gone to the doctor for the annual physical required by his company expecting nothing and feeling fine—only to find out he had black lung. The doctors told him he might have five years to live.

I remember it vividly even now, the pain I felt as the entire landscape of my father's life suddenly came into view: a man raised outdoors with a love of nature, forced underground and away from the light by the Depression, the immediate demands of feeding a family postponing then eliminating any hope he had of getting an education. I remember pondering the ironic tragedy of a man who had never smoked so much as one cigarette in his life acquiring emphysema—a disease most commonly associated with heavy smokers.

"I'm telling you this not because I want to scare you," he said, "but because you know how important education is to me. It looks like I'm not going to be here to help you. I want you to promise me that somehow you will find a way to do what I couldn't do and finish your education."

This was the defining moment of my life. In that instant, Father's hopes and dreams became mine.

There was no choice, of course, no possible response other than, "I will." And so I made that solemn commitment with fear and trepidation, not knowing how I would be able to do what no one in my family had ever done before.

Through the grace of God and the abundant opportunities provided by this country, I was able to keep my promise. I won a scholarship to George Washington University. The day I graduated from high school I left the small mining community in southeastern Utah where I was raised for Washington, D.C. I never returned.

Instead, I began working at the United States Senate while I went to college and law school. After school and a brief stint in the U.S. Army, I returned to the Senate, where I became involved in the Congressional Oversight Committee. For fifteen years as an investigator, chief investigator, counsel, director of oversight and, ultimately, staff director of a congressional committee, I turned over rocks for the Senate, looking for the scum of the earth.

I found people posing as doctors who had never gone to medical school, dentists who drilled holes in healthy teeth to create cavities they could fill at public expense, nursing home owners who abused the people they were supposed to care for, clinical laboratories that performed "sink tests"—literally pouring the medical samples they gathered down the drain or flushing them down the toilet to spare the expense of testing them properly—and a host of other creative criminals.

An activist by nature, I posed as a Medicaid patient for a year, visiting clinics across the country to test the quality of medical care provided to the poor. I went undercover and carried a wire in a joint investigation with the U.S. Attorney in New York, chased crooks and corrupt politicians in Chicago, and danced with the Mafia more times than I can remember.

Along the way, I was taken for a ride by a wise guy with a gun in a shoulder holster and threatened by high-priced lawyers. I was offered bribes and "soft" money, had my home burglarized, my phone tapped, and my car nearly torched. Nevertheless, I took great pleasure in shining the light on the vultures who feed at public expense and take advantage of the taxpayer and the poor and disabled. To this day, I still get some satisfaction in knowing that over the years we recovered millions of dollars, saved billions of dollars, and helped put a lot of bad guys out of business and in jail.

But despite our success, I found myself growing increasingly sad and cynical. The problems we "solved" kept recurring. The scope of the crimes we were investigating kept growing. I couldn't help feeling that we were winning a lot of battles but losing the war.

Finally, in 1985 I came to the conclusion that the "top down" remedies I had pursued in Congress did not work. Long-term change, the only kind that can be sustained, always comes from the bottom up. Such is the nature of a democracy.

With this in mind, I did a 180. I decided to look for the best instead of the worst and began what I have since referred to as a magnificent odyssey, searching for the heart of America. Taking a lead from Dr. Albert Schweitzer, who observed, "Example isn't the best way to teach, it is the only way," I began looking for people who represented the best of our society, the best instincts of man, and the best part of ourselves.

The people profiled in this book emerged from this process. They come from all walks of life and all ages, representing a cross section of the richness and diversity of America. While each of these individuals is remarkable in their own right, what is most remarkable is the collective testimony they offer to the enduring vitality of America's core values.

Ever since September 11, 2001, and the launch of the war on terrorism, increasing attention has been focused on our values. But these events only exposed a need that has long been evident.

Twelve years earlier in his farewell address, President Ronald Reagan expressed this concern in the great tradition of warnings in Presidential farewells. At a time when he could have addressed many other issues, President Reagan chose to focus on the need for "an informed patriotism" in our country.

"Those of us who are over thirty-five or so years of age grew up in a different America," President Reagan said. "We were taught, very directly, what it means to be an American. And we absorbed, almost in the air, a love of country and an appreciation of its institutions."

Later, President Bill Clinton echoed Reagan's concern. "Beyond all else, our country is a set of convictions," Clinton said in one of his last speeches before he left office. "We hold these truths to be self evident: that all men are created equal; that they are endowed by their Creator with certain inalienable rights; that among these are life, liberty and the pursuit of happiness. Our whole history can be seen first as an effort to preserve these rights and then as an effort to make them real in the lives of all of our citizens."

In his inaugural address, President George W. Bush, Clinton's successor in office, eloquently expressed the same beliefs, reminding us "America has been united across generations by grand and enduring ideals."

What are these enduring ideals? What are America's core values? What makes us successful as individuals and as a nation?

To date, the most comprehensive and penetrating answer comes from Alexis de Tocqueville's classic study, *On*

Democracy in America. De Tocqueville came to the United States in 1831. "Near enough," he said, "to the time when the states of America were founded to be accurately acquainted with their elements, and sufficiently removed from that period to judge some of the results."

De Tocqueville brought with him the perspective of an aristocrat and the detachment of a foreigner. His observations of the character of our society have stood the test of time and become the reference point for all subsequent analysis. No one since has defined the genius of America as well.

The Heart of America: Ten Core Values that Make Our Country Great begins where de Tocqueville concluded, examining the application and utility of America's core values in our contemporary world. Each chapter of this book focuses on one of the ten core values de Tocqueville identified and which are still relevant to our world today: Compassion, Opportunity, Responsibility, Equality, Valor, Ambition, Liberty, Unity, Enterprise and Spirituality.

Each section is introduced with a short essay that explains how these values form the foundation of democracy in America and why they continue to be important. Then the enduring nature of each value is illustrated with the stories of real people who show us how we can instill these values in our own lives.

While these people are identified with the specific value they best exemplify, they each make the broader point that our core values do not exist independent of each other. They are interrelated and inextricably connected.

Oprah Winfrey, for example, provides a wonderful illustration of the enduring nature of opportunity in America. Few have traveled a greater distance than she has, from her humble beginnings to her current position as one of the most influential women in the world. But that journey would not have been possible if she did not have in significant degree many of the other core values identified in this book, including ambition, enterprise, valor, compassion and spirituality. The same can be said for each of the other individuals used as illustrations.

This book has been organized so you can read it straight through or bounce around as you like. I encourage you to read it thoughtfully. Pick it up and read a chapter before bed or in a quiet moment of reflection. As you do, consider the importance of each of these values in your own life. Share it with your families and talk about it with your friends.

Ultimately, this book is about you and how you and people like you make this country what it is. This is your book. You are the heart of America.

America is as bad as the worst among us and as good as the best. Ultimately, the greatness of America is a reflection of the greatness of its people—a diverse people representational of all aspects of humanity, liberated to find the fullest expression of their hopes and dreams.

The genius of America is that the core values that make our country great are the same values that define our success as individuals. That is why America is always a work in progress. America is becoming. America is a promise. America is an ideal to cherish and a dream to pursue.

America began with a claim of responsibility and recognition—the declaration "We the people." Then and now, the best measure of America is the sum of its people.

America is great and will be greater to the exact degree we as individuals honor our past, follow our dreams and live up to our responsibility. It is my hope that *The Heart of America: Ten Core Values that Make Our Country Great* will feed this process and serve as a reminder of the mantle we have inherited, the sacrifices that have been made for the liberties we enjoy and our ongoing challenge to continue to form "a more perfect union."

One

COMPASSION

★ ★ ★ ★

*America is great because
America is good; America will cease
to be great when it is no longer good.*

Alexis de Tocqueville

★ ★ ★ ★

I f you want to find hope in Anacostia, you have to bring it with you. Anacostia is just across the river yet worlds away from the rest of Washington, D.C. For the most part, Washington is a place where people come to pursue their dreams. Anacostia is a place where dreams die early. Poverty is bone-deep in Anacostia. Most of the students in the public schools there are at risk. More than three fourths of these students read below basic proficiency levels and are considered functionally illiterate.

For several years now, my wife Angela and I have visited schools in Anacostia on a regular basis, bringing exemplary young people with us and asking them to inspire their peers and give them hope. One of the schools we have repeatedly visited is Moten Elementary School.

Five years ago, when we learned that many of the students at Moten would go without at Christmas, my wife and I felt compelled to go shopping. We went to a mall near where we live, found a toy store that would give us a discount, and filled garbage bags with over five hundred toys. We wanted to make sure every student at

Moten would have at least one present to mark the holiday.

We repeated this exercise the following year, inviting friends from the Heart of America to join us. But the third year, with a better understanding of what the school's needs were, we decided that instead of buying the kids toys for Christmas we would bring them books. When we arrived at Moten that year, we found the principal had asked some of her best students to help us unload. One of these kids was an eager young man named Darius whose eyes lit up when he saw what we brought. His response was so engaging, we felt compelled to ask him to pick a book we could read together.

To our surprise, the book he picked was one we brought for the kids in preschool. It was painful to watch this obviously bright fifth-grader stumble through a book my wife and I had read to our son when he was three years old.

Any parent knows that once you have a child of your own, you can never again look at a child in need the same way. I watched tears of compassion well up in my wife's eyes as Darius read.

In the background, we could hear faculty members rehearsing the song "Eye on the Sparrow" in preparation for the school assembly that would soon follow the presentation of books, their voices blending together, rising above and mixing with the lone voice of this one child. In that moment, I felt a father's despair for a child who may be left behind, a child who may be lost before he has really had a chance to begin. At the same time, my spirits were lifted by the hope provided by the voices in harmony and the knowledge that such beauty can be created whenever people come together for some good purpose.

Compassion means to "suffer with." When you touch

someone's pain from a distance, and in fear, it becomes pity. Compassion comes when you share someone's suffering and touch their pain with love. When you do not run away from pain but walk toward it with compassion you bring healing and strength.

Compassion is man's highest attribute. Most of even our best instincts have a base side. Love, hope, faith, courage and loyalty can all be corrupted by ego, selfishness, and human frailty, transformed into doubt, fear and hate. True compassion stands alone, unyielding.

Compassion is the bridge between us. It connects our lives by a thousand sympathetic threads. We all need to exercise our compassion and find support in the compassion of others.

At its essence compassion is the difference between saying, "I am my brother's keeper" and "I am my brother." In Darius's case, it was the inspiration for a national program that has since distributed millions of dollars of books to children in need across the country.

Compassion in America has spiritual roots. It is anchored in unity and equality and expressed in opportunity and responsibility. It is a value as old as civilization itself—adapted, perfected and structured by the founding fathers to fulfill the promise of a new land.

Five centuries before Christ, Sophocles observed that "kindness begets kindness." Later, in Rome, Tertullian observed, "He who lives only to benefit himself confers on the world a benefit when he dies."

The Judeo-Christian heritage extended and elevated the value of compassion. Among the Hebrews, honoring God, caring for family and helping neighbors were central values. The Hebrew word for giving is *tzedek*, which literally means "justice" and is the motivating force for *tzedakah*—acts of righteousness.

Through the generations, from culture to culture,

religion to religion, Moses to Mohammed, Buddha to Christ, whenever men ask the fundamental question of existence, the answer is the same. The Torah reminds us, "Deeds of love are worth as much as all the commandments of the law." Followers of Islam are taught, "Whatever good you do for others, you send before your own soul and shall find with God, who sees all you do." The religions of the East—Hinduism and Buddhism—express the same thought with their admonition to "hurt none by word or deed and be consistent in your well-doing."

Christians are bound to "love one another as I have loved you." The Gospel of Luke records the deeds of the Good Samaritan, who went out of his way to aid anyone in need of assistance. His example became the Christian model for compassion and was cited in the fourth century as an example by Saint Jerome, who commended a woman he knew, noting, "She preferred to store her money in the stomach of the needy rather than in her purse."

The founders of the American republic were schooled in this philosophy and animated by their Christian faith. They established compassion as the rock on which the Bill of Rights, the free enterprise system and democracy rest. Compassion is the central value in our social, economic and political systems. Without it, our society would self-destruct.

When asked to sum up his observations of America, Alexis de Tocqueville is said to have said, "America is great because America is good. America will cease to be great when it is no longer good."

Early in our nation's history, compassion in America was obvious, manifested in each occasion neighbors gathered to help each other—to do together what an individual family could not then do alone: raise a barn, dig a well or harvest a crop. Later, pioneers banded together for mutual protection and support. In the darkest days of our nation during the Civil War, a new manifestation of compassion came as thousands of women volunteered to nurse the wounded, the sick and the dying.

"Although sad at the office we performed," one of them wrote, "our hearts were filled with pleasure in the work we were doing. . . . Those to whom I ministered seemed to me more like brothers than strangers."

The truth that nurse found in her work during the Civil War, thousands of others have found on a daily basis in the years since: giving is receiving.

"It is one of the most beautiful compensations of this life," Emerson wrote, "that no man can sincerely try to help another without helping himself."

From the perspective of society, compassion works to advance common interests. At the close of World War II, General George C. Marshall recognized this fact in designing the Marshall Plan. "Our policy is directed not against any country or doctrine," he said, "but against hunger, poverty, desperation and chaos."

Marshall, who was distantly related to the former Chief Justice of the U.S. Supreme Court, John Marshall, served in the military with distinction until he "retired" in November 1945. Two years later, President Truman named him Secretary of State.

The Marshall Plan he developed in this capacity is seen as a premier example of national compassion. The plan committed the United States to a broad program designed to reduce the hunger, homelessness, sickness and political restlessness of the 270 million people in sixteen nations ravaged by war in Western Europe. It cost the American taxpayer $13.3 billion. Adjusted for inflation, this is equivalent to giving five times more than all of our current foreign aid programs.

In 1953, George C. Marshall received the Nobel Peace Prize in Oslo, Norway, for this effort. Appropriately, he accepted it not as his individual triumph, but as a representative of the American people, whose faith and commitment had made the program a success.

Since then, other programs such as Food for Peace, the Agency for International Development and the Peace Corps have flowed from the heart of America. The Peace Corps is particularly notable since it is an all-volunteer effort that requires a substantial commitment from individual American citizens. Since 1961, 168,000 people have joined the Peace Corps, 95 percent of them college graduates. Each of these people has given two years of their lives to make things better in the 136 countries the Peace Corps has aided around the world.

No one has expressed the rationale for compassionate action more clearly than Albert Einstein. Einstein was one of millions who fled Europe when Hitler came to power. He took up permanent residence in the United States in 1932 and became an American citizen in 1940.

Shortly before his death, Einstein was interviewed by the editor of a scientific publication. The interview ranged across the breadth of Einstein's work, including the mysteries of quantum physics and his attempt to read the mind of God and develop a unifying theory for the universe.

As they were wrapping up, the interviewer said he had one final question.

"Why are we here?" he asked.

When Einstein did not immediately reply, the interviewer became embarrassed and apologized for asking something so difficult.

Einstein smiled gently.

"If I looked puzzled," he said, "it is because you asked me something so simple. We are here to serve one another."

Few understand this principle as well as the people whose stories follow. Only a person with infinite compassion, like Bob Macauley, could generate billions of dollars in life-saving aid for millions of people in need and still be able to focus with equal intensity on the desperate need of a child half a world away he has never met. Only a Macauley, when that child was lost, would be so moved as to send a tanker full of chocolate to the children of his homeland in his memory.

Aaron Feuerstein became a symbol of what the average worker would like corporate America to be at time when America's faith in corporate America was at an all-time low. Feuerstein took $25 million out of his pocket after a devastating fire destroyed his textile mill to pay his employees' salaries until they could return to work. His explanation is simple: "It was the right thing to do."

Trevor Armbrister reinvented the pioneer tradition of "barn-raising" to give relevance to that rural tradition in our urban times, while Rita Schiavone took a simple act of compassion — cooking a hot meal for an elderly neighbor — and turned it into a network that provides a million meals a year for shut-ins in and around Philadelphia.

By far the youngest, Amber Coffman is perhaps the most remarkable. Beginning at age eight, Amber has helped the homeless, starting her own organization at eleven. She fed over 30,000 people and served over 350,000 meals before going off to college. When she graduates, she says, she wants to buy a house for the homeless so they can live together.

What these people suggest is that perhaps the most selfish thing we can do is to be selfless. Compassion is a reflection of the most fundamental fact of life. As individuals, and as a society built around individuals, we need each other.

On the 150th anniversary of the Constitutional

Convention, Franklin Delano Roosevelt captured this
sentiment when he said, "In every land there are always
at work forces that drive men apart and forces that draw
men together. In our personal ambitions we are individuals. But in our seeking for economic and political
progress as a nation, we all go up, or else we all go
down, as one people."

For Bob, Rita, Alan, Trevor and Amber it is more
simple. As Trevor says, "It just comes down to love."

★ ★ ★ ★

Robert C. Macauley

"This lovely poem was a favorite of our son, Marek," Andrze Skabon wrote Bob Macauley in December of 1982.

This we already know
For it is always the same,
With the frost and the snow
Come the Holidays.
Already the tables are groaning,
Animals speak to us with human voices
Saying, nothing on this earth
Can separate one heart from another
For the Holidays are coming.

When he had come to Bob's attention two years before, Marek had what was thought to be an inoperable brain tumor. For five years the doctors in his native Poland had done what they could for the boy with their limited resources. Finally, they decided there was nothing more they could do and gave up.

In desperation, the family and turned to the church. There they heard about a man in America who had started an organization called AmeriCares that was sending badly needed medicine and medical supplies to Poland—then still under martial law

With faint hope, Marek's father sent a letter to Robert C. Macauley, founder of AmeriCares, pleading for whatever help he could provide. To Andrze's surprise, the man in America, a man he had never met or spoken with, arranged to have his son flown to London for the sophisticated surgery he needed.

Bob found a surgeon who had had success in similar cases and pressed him for assistance. Four operations and several months later, the happy and healthy child returned home to his family.

But tragedy sometimes compounds tragedy. A few months after his return, the boy had a bicycle accident severe enough to land him back in the hospital.

"We were saddened to learn that you had taken a fall from your bicycle," Bob wrote Marek in August 1982 when he heard the news. "But I hope and pray that all is going well for you now."

The letter continued in this extraordinary way: "Marek, whether you know it or not, you have been unofficially adopted by my family and by me. How seldom it is that anyone is afforded the opportunity of trying to help a fine young man such as you. For that privilege, we will be eternally grateful. I just wanted you to know that you have our love and are in our prayers every evening."

Sadly, three months later, Marek died.

"During Marek's illness, he was exceptionally good and cheerful," his father wrote. "We had to thrust our care upon him, as he never asked for anything. . . . Although he lived barely eleven years, he performed on this earth an important task—he made us aware that the long road of life had but one ending, that in life we must remember to give all of ourselves to Him, so that we may ultimately be joined with Him. That is why we do not despair. We will always remember you, sir, who demonstrated so much heart, so much goodness and help for our little boy. We will always ask for God's blessing and care for you and your family."

By the time Macauley received Andrze's letter, the holidays had arrived. He found himself thinking about the boy and his father. "The holidays are coming . . . " Marek's poem read.

If I were a Polish father, Bob wondered, suffering under

political repression and martial law, with no money and little food, living in a country where everything is rationed—what little token of love could I give my child? He saw a box of chocolates someone had sent him and had an inspiration. There was no chocolate in Poland.

The next morning, Macauley called the president of Hershey's Chocolate and told his story.

"I told him what I was trying to do and asked him if he could help me out a little," he recalls.

The man from Hershey said, "I will give you a million kisses."

From there, he went to the Mars candy company. At first Mars did not respond as well, but then Bob mentioned Hershey's had already committed it's participation in a big way.

"How much?" Mars asked.

Bob said, "A million," without saying a million what.

"We will match that," Mars said.

Macauley followed up with Nestle and Peter Paul Cadbury. By the following Monday—three days after his inspiration—165,000 pounds of chocolate were on the way to Poland.

Each container carried the label "From the children of America to the children of Poland, with love." In Marek's honor, the shipments continued every Christmas for three more years.

In presenting AmeriCares with the President's Volunteer Action Award two years later, President Ronald Reagan took great delight in telling the story of Bob's chocolate for Poland.

"Next time you go to Poland," the president said with his characteristic good humor, "you may want to take a dentist along."

★ ★ ★ ★

Rita Ungaro-Schiavone

Thirty years ago, Rita Ungaro-Schiavone stopped by a neighbor's house to visit. She was concerned because the woman was a widow and lived alone. Still, she was unprepared for what she saw.

"What I saw was an elderly woman, slightly built, sitting on the side of the bed," Rita said. "Her legs were dangling, and you could tell they were atrophied from disuse."

The shades were drawn and it was dark, but the lady didn't seem to mind. Rita chatted with her for a while and learned the woman had crippling arthritis. She had lost most of her vision and was nearly catatonic with depression.

It was summer and the room was hot and stuffy. There was no air conditioning, not even a fan to circulate the oppressive air.

When Rita went into the kitchen to get the woman something cold to drink, she noted there was some dog food, but no dog in sight. There was no milk, soda, juice or bread in the refrigerator.

Her neighbor stayed on her mind as she prepared dinner for her family that evening. On instinct, she decided to make an extra portion for her new friend.

"I was preparing a nice, nourishing meal for my family," Rita remembers. "I thought I would share what we were having with her, rather than give her some canned goods she probably would never use."

Twenty-five years later, a network of 15,000 volunteers called Aid for Friends has evolved from that simple, human instinct. They do what Rita once did alone. Some cook; some carry; some deliver and visit; some do all three. But they all work without cost or compensation. Together, they provide more than a million meals a year to people in need in and around Philadelphia.

"I really didn't know I was starting a program," Rita said. "It just happened."

The first food center was set up in Rita's house. Within ten years, there were more than three dozen. The first Aid for Friends storage center was her freezer. That one freezer became 20, then 50, and finally grew to more than 70 freezers and walk-in boxes before operations were consolidated four years ago. Now Aid for Friends operates out of a 30,000-square-foot warehouse with two giant walk-in freezers that can accommodate enough food to nourish the elderly and disabled for weeks.

Once petrified to speak at her son's PTA, Rita has now spoken to more than 400,000 people. She has recruited volunteers from nearly 300 churches and synagogues.

Rita's goal is to help shut-ins maintain their independence and to allow them to remain home as long as possible. Her message is simple: Everyone can do something.

"If you don't want to cook, you share your financial resources; you share your time; you drive and deliver; or you share a part of yourself as a visitor," she says. "If you cook, you just put a little aside. That's not much extra, not much effort. But just one meal adds up fast."

When I asked her what she has learned from all this, Rita said, "People have to realize they have power. God gave them power. We have the power to do things and change things. We can change people's lives."

"Through it all, " Rita says, "I found out this was what I was supposed to do with my life. I wasn't supposed to use all my spare time just swimming or ice skating or enjoying myself. And my life has meaning beyond my wildest imagination."

★ ★ ★ ★

Aaron Feuerstein

You don't have to look hard to find another story about corporate greed. The papers are full of articles about executives who have made a fortune for themselves while driving their companies into bankruptcy and costing employees their jobs and sometimes their life savings. The single-minded pursuit of self-interest has shaken the public confidence and brought much of corporate America into disrepute.

In the midst of all these scandals, one man, Aaron Feuerstein, has stood tall. If Enron and Tyco have come to symbolize what's wrong with corporate America, Feuerstein and his company, Malden Mills, stand for what's right.

On December 11, 1995, Feuerstein celebrated his seventieth birthday at his favorite restaurant—Cafe Budapest in Boston. He returned home to find his phone ringing. He had no way to know it had been ringing for hours.

When he picked up the receiver, he learned there was a fire at Malden Mills. The company his grandfather had founded at the turn of the century was dying.

Malden Mills is the company that developed Polartec, a popular clothing material. Known for its soft texture, warmth, light weight and sturdy resistance to wind and weather—while made predominately from recycled plastic soda bottles—it was one of the few products embraced with equal enthusiasm by outdoorsmen and environmentalists alike. The company's customers read like a catalogue of catalogues: Lands End, L. L. Bean, Eddie Bauer, the North Face and Patagonia.

As a result, Malden Mills had profited when others in the textile industry were struggling. Now it seemed to be coming to an end. Over 100 textile plants had closed in 1995, laying off thousands of employees. It looked like Malden Mills and its 3,000 employees were about to join their ranks.

When Feuerstein reached the plant, he found one of the ten largest industrial fires ever recorded in the United States and the worst fire in Massachusetts in a century. Seven brick and wood-frame buildings, some 600,000 square feet of manufacturing space, were ablaze. One by one, they were consumed by the fire and collapsed.

While others were in tears, Aaron did not cry. "Weeping is a way of feeling sorry for yourself," he told CBS *60 Minutes.* "You can't think creatively when weeping. The only thing that went through my mind was, How can I recreate the mill?"

While the fire continued to blaze, Feuerstein made a decision many others in the textile industry still find hard to believe. Since his family owned the company, he could have pocketed $300 million in insurance and retired. Instead, Feuerstein announced he would rebuild the mill right where the old one had stood. More than that, he said, he felt he had an obligation to his employees.

No one quite knew what that meant, so two days later Feuerstein called a meeting to explain what he had in mind. Malden Mills' employees, their friends and families, as well as most of the community the mill supported, gathered in a high school gymnasium to hear what he had to say.

Feuerstein stood alone at the front of the room. Without any fanfare, he said, "I will get right to my announcement. For the next thirty days, our employees will be paid their full salaries." He went on to say the traditional Christmas bonus of $275 would also be paid, just as in prior years. Health care coverage would be continued, as would all other benefits.

"But over and above the money," he said, "the most important thing Malden Mills can do is to get you back to work." He said he expected operations to resume by January 2 and for the plant to be in full operation within 90 days.

Then, turning to the reporters present, he said pointedly, "We are going to continue to operate in Lawrence. We had the opportunity to run south many years ago. We didn't do it then, and we are not going to do it now."

With that, the room exploded. Afterwards, one of the workers told NBC, "I've never seen so many grown men cry in my life. We thought our jobs were gone."

Shocked as some might have been by what Aaron said, many were even more surprised by what he did. He kept his word.

By the end of December, 10 percent of Malden Mills workforce was already back to work. A month later, 65 percent of the workers had returned. With the advent of spring, less than four months after the fire, Malden Mills was operating at full capacity.

Feuerstein spent the $300 million the insurance company gave him and then borrowed $100 million more to build a new plant that was both environment-friendly and worker-friendly. He also paid out more than $25 million in salaries, carrying employees month-to-month until they could all return to work.

"I think it was a wise business decision, but that isn't why I did it," Feuerstein says. "I did it because it was the right thing to do."

Asked to explain what he meant at a conference on business and ethics at MIT, Feuerstein said, "I remember as a young boy, five or six years old, sitting at my father's table and hearing him say that my grandfather always insisted on paying his workers before sunset. He felt it was a sin to oppress the poor and needy and that it was important to treat people the way we expect them to treat us."

Feuerstein's interpretation of the Golden Rule meant, "I had to rebuild. There was no way I was going to take 3,000 people and throw them in the streets. And there is no way that I should be the one to condemn that community, which has suffered so much in the Twentieth Century, to economic oblivion. No, sir."

Not surprisingly, Feuerstein's actions attracted a lot of attention. ABC named him "Person of the Week." NBC said he was the "first boss of America" and a "saint for the nineties." *60 Minutes* called him "The Mensch of Malden Mills" and a shining example of compassion.

"Everything I did after the fire was in keeping with the ethical standards I've tried to maintain my entire life," Aaron responds, "so it is surprising we've gotten so much attention. Whether I deserve it not, I guess I became a symbol of what the average worker would like corporate America to be in a time when the American dream has been pretty badly injured."

★ ★ ★ ★

Trevor Armbrister is a senior staff editor for *Reader's Digest*. While covering a story in Midland, Texas, in the 1980s this veteran reporter had a very unjournalistic experience.

Like most American communities, Midland has a large number of elderly and handicapped citizens with incomes so limited they cannot afford to repair their aging houses. A retired oil scout named Bobby Trimble decided to do something about it.

Trimble organized his friends and neighbors and gathered them for an old-fashioned "barn-raising" one day in April. The day was such a success, Trimble and his friends decided to make it an annual event and began coming together each April thereafter to renovate some of the dilapidated houses around them.

Trimble and the more experienced members of the team scouted each location, assessed the need, and obtained the necessary building materials—often at no charge—from participating corporations in the community. Then, on the chosen day, a small army of volunteers arrived at each work site in the morning. When they left at the end of the day, the run-down houses were magically restored.

"It's like Christmas in April," one elderly woman said after watching her neighbors transform her house, at once expressing her awe and giving the program a name.

Trevor had been a writer and editor with the *Digest, Saturday Evening Post* and a number of other publications for more than thirty years. He had been trained to be dispassionate and objective. Yet there was something about this program he could not get out of his mind.

"When I went to Midland," Trevor says, "I didn't know anything about home repair. I had never tried to repair a home and couldn't have told you the difference between a plumb line and a deadline. These things just aren't in my background. But I thought the idea of amassing an army, literally an army of compassion, to attack some of the problems we face in the community was worth looking at."

What he found was more impressive and inspirational than anything he might have imagined.

"I'd done my research and seen the numbers, but that didn't prepare me for what I saw," he says. "I saw Midland become a beehive of activity. For one day, everyone seemed to come together. There were people wearing Christmas in April T-shirts everywhere. Class distinctions, occupational distinctions and racial separations all seemed to vanish because everybody in Midland—at least for that one day—seemed concerned about one thing—helping a neighbor in need."

Before he knew it, Trevor found himself involved. He asked Trimble's permission to start a chapter of Christmas in April in Washington, D.C., and when that proved a stunning success, he was inspired to create Christmas in April USA, an umbrella group founded to seed and support the development of similar programs in other communities.

"Trevor is definitely not a builder . . . in the sense of carpentry," Trimble has said of his friend, "but he is a builder in the sense that he gets people together to get things done."

Soon there were chapters of Christmas in April in every state in the union. By the time he retired as chairman of the board of Christmas in April USA and turned over the reins to other willing hands, over 100,000 volunteers were participating in this annual event, making a contribution said to have a market value in excess of $8 million.

But the benefit is far beyond that.

"When I was a young man living in New York," Trevor

explains, "I lived in the suburbs and commuted to work. I would get on the railroad and ride in a metal cocoon through Harlem and other poor parts of town. Later, when I covered the civil rights advances of the 1960s, I remember going to the houses of the poor in the South and listening to their stories. I was listening to their rhetoric, but I wasn't really hearing what they had to say. I was focused on the story of their struggle for equal rights. Now, for the first time, I was able to open my eyes and see these people, black and white, as my neighbors. I was able to see the conditions they cope with and empathize with them. You can't put a price tag on that."

It is more than a little ironic that a man who has lived in many countries around the world, written five books—two of them bestsellers—and ghost-written for two presidents, a man who, in his own words, has always been petrified at the thought of changing a light bulb, now finds his greatest satisfaction as a community builder.

"It's taught me," Trevor concludes, "that what I do has to be measured on a bigger scale. I used to think my worth would be measured by how good my articles are. But this experience has led me to believe that there is something a lot bigger out there.

"It comes down to love. Everybody wants to be involved, but many people don't know how or what they can do. I have learned there are a lot of ways love can be expressed if you look for them. This is just one vehicle."

★ ★ ★ ★

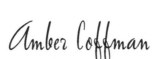

In 1995, I attended a rather unusual birthday party. The party was for Amber Coffman, a remarkable young lady who was then about to turn twelve.

Instead of someone's living room, the party was held in the American Legion hall in Glen Burnie, Maryland. Though it was her birthday, Amber made it clear the guests of honor were the homeless people she served. The handwritten invitations she distributed invited us to come and celebrate with her, but rather than bringing gifts for her she asked us to bring something for the homeless instead.

Amber began volunteering at the age of eight at a homeless shelter she visited with her mom. By the time she was ten, she knew she wanted to do something more and set up her own organization—Happy Helpers for the Homeless.

"I am drawn to the homeless," Amber says, "because I'm the daughter of a single mother, and things haven't always been easy for us."

When Amber says it hasn't always been easy for her, it is more than a bit of an understatement. She has never met her father. Her mother, Bobbi, has always struggled financially, sometimes working three jobs to make ends meet but too proud to go on welfare. Welfare, she says, is for people who can't work. Bobbi is more than willing to work—though work is often hard to find.

"I had a dream that I could find a way to help the homeless," Amber says, "but I knew I couldn't provide shelter so I tried to come up with something doable. That's when I hit on lunches."

At first, Amber spent days soliciting donations from grocery stores and restaurants around her hometown. She asked everyone she could think of for donations of food to make bag lunches.

"Most of the owners didn't take me seriously or were worried about being liable if someone got sick," she recalls.

Others, like the owner of her neighborhood McDonald's, interviewed the ten-year-old girl at great length to see if she was sincere. He was convinced and agreed to help.

When they began Happy Helpers, it was just the two of them—Amber and her mom. They made fifty sandwiches. By the second week, it was 100. By the third week as word spread, it was 200. Now, a small battalion of volunteers—mostly teens—come to Amber's apartment every Saturday morning and turns the living room into a fast food factory.

Together they assemble 700 sandwiches every weekend, for a total of 36,400 a year. They give away at least as many doughnuts and pastries, plus thousands of gallons of juice, Kool-Aid and water. At least once a month, toiletries and clothing are gathered through neighborhood donations.

McDonald's provides buns, cheese, mustard and paper cups. Mrs. Fields, BJ's and other local businesses contribute as well. A nearby 7-Eleven lets Amber use its refrigerator for storage.

Sandwiches are delivered locally every Saturday afternoon, but the majority are stored for distribution at predesignated locations where the street people gather in Baltimore every Sunday morning. Almost invariably, the homeless are lined up and waiting for Amber when she arrives.

To date, Amber has helped feed over 30,000 people, many of them women and children. She has served over 350,000 meals and started seven chapters of Happy Helpers in Maryland. Her program has been replicated in forty-nine of the fifty states.

"The truth is," Amber says, "anyone can be homeless. All it

takes is a little bad luck or getting laid off from a job."

Once you hit the streets, she has learned, it can be hard to recover. "You have no home, no transportation, nothing to eat. To get a job again, you need clean clothes, a place to bathe and a way to get to work."

Among the rewards she treasures most is the memory of the middle-aged man who approached her three years back to simply say "Thank you." He told her, "I have a job now and a place to live. I couldn't have done it without you."

Another strong memory is the man who said he would have starved to death that winter if it weren't for her help. "When the snow came, everyone else stayed home," the man recalled. "But you were here every Sunday, rain or shine."

Among her more tangible rewards are the thousands of dollars she has won in awards and scholarships. She has also become something of a celebrity, appearing on *CBS This Morning, The Today Show, Montel Williams,* and *Oprah.* She has been featured in *People, Seventeen, Reader's Digest, Parade* and numerous other publications.

Two years ago she even won a contest—beating 10,000 candidates nominated by children—that led to her identification as Crayola Crayons' Ultimate True Blue Hero. Her name is now emblazoned on the side of a dark blue crayon Crayola created in her honor.

Amber was a featured speaker at the President's Summit for America that created America's Promise and serves on the Maryland Governor's Commission on Service. Last fall, she received a Presidential Appointment, becoming the youngest member of the Council on Service and Civic Participation. In this capacity, Amber has spoken to thousands of young adults considering community service. Her advice is always the same.

"Once you start, it's really easy," she says. "All you need is time and love to share. Once you get into it, you will find it is really rewarding."

While hunger and the homeless remain her focus, Amber

has found time to volunteer with some forty other charitable organizations, including the National Multiple Sclerosis Society, Special Olympics, the National Kidney Foundation and a host of local programs.

"There are urgent needs to be met, and I feel compelled to meet them," Amber explains. "It's just something that is inside of me; it is why I am here on earth."

Amber is currently at Pepperdine University on a full scholarship. When she graduates, she hopes to join the Peace Corps. But her dream is to have enough money to buy a house for homeless families.

"We will call it Happy Helpers for the Homeless House," she says, "and every day we'd all sit down for family dinner together."

Two

OPPORTUNITY

★ ★ ★ ★

America is another name for opportunity.

Ralph Waldo Emerson

★ ★ ★ ★

America is the land of opportunity.

One hundred years before the *Mayflower,* the French had already begun looking for fame and fortune in the New World, working the cod banks off Nova Scotia. The Spaniards, led by the Italian Christopher Columbus, were not far behind.

A full eight inches taller than the average Spaniard of his day, with flowing red hair and exuberant ways, Columbus must have looked as odd as his notion of sailing west to deliver a letter to the Grand Khan of China sounded. The voyage was thought to be impractical, dangerous and expensive.

"Everyone to whom I spoke of this enterprise thought it a mere jest," he said.

But the promise of El Dorado was enticing enough that Queen Isabella and King Ferdinand were finally persuaded to finance an exploratory expedition. On August 2, 1492, Columbus and his crew went on board for confession and set sail with the tide "for gospel and for gold."

Columbus and his crew sailed through August and September, across what was then called the Sea of

Gloom, without finding any of the islands they expected. As they entered October, his crew and the captains of the other two ships begged him to turn back.

On October 11, Columbus wrote in his ship's log he "prayed mightily to the Lord." The following day he sighted land, now known as San Salvador in the Bahamas. From there, Columbus went on to explore Haiti and Cuba before heading back to tell what he had found, bringing with him samples of spice and gold.

His patrons were so impressed that Columbus was given a fleet of seventeen ships for his second voyage. Rumors of gold leaked out and a desperate rush of would-be adventurers besieged him for space on his ships.

"Not a man," Columbus said, "down to the very tailors, does not beg to be allowed to become a discoverer."

About 100 years later, the British celebrated the return of Sir Francis Drake from an expedition that had taken him to Brazil, Chile and Peru. Drake brought back so much plunder his flagship could barely list into port. His success fueled the vision of a New World of unbounded virgin land and untold riches. As a result, the London Company, a commercial trading company, financed a British expedition to America. Intent on settling to the north of the Spanish and the south of the French, they came up the Chesapeake Bay and entered the James River in modern Virginia. With that, the longest and most determined gold rush in history began, but it would not find full expression until the Republic was formed and the power of the people unleashed.

"The discovery of America opened a thousand new paths to fortune, and led obscure adventurers to wealth and power," de Tocqueville would say of that time. "In America, every one finds facilities unknown elsewhere for maintaining or increasing his fortune. The spirit of gain is always on the stretch."

The pursuit of happiness is one of the inalienable rights upon which this country rests. In the words of James Adams, "The whole American Dream has been based on the chance to get ahead, for one's self or one's children."

Opportunity comes from liberty and is made possible by equality. When fed by ambition and sustained by courage, the pursuit of happiness has limitless possibilities.

At the same time, we must recognize the happiness of some has always been purchased at the expense of others. It is a story as old and shameful as our treatment of Native Americans and as recent as the current plague of corporate greed. There are always those who cannot see beyond their immediate personal interests and have no concern for the broader consequences of their actions.

Though they compel our attention, fill our courts and challenge our sense of justice, these people are the exception and not the rule. Intuitively, most people know the single-minded pursuit of self-interest can not be sustained in a democracy. It corrodes the foundation on which it rests.

America is the first nation in the history of the world to be founded with a purpose. The great phrases that frame our society and support that purpose still resonate today. They remind us of who we are, what we stand for and what we will die for.

In the words of Lyndon B. Johnson, they are "a promise to every citizen that he shall share in the dignity of man. This dignity cannot be found in man's possession; it cannot be found in his power, or his position. It really rests on his right to be treated as a man equal in opportunity to all others."

To de Tocqueville's aristocratic eyes, the spectacle of men and women liberated to make their own destiny must have seemed a bit unsettling.

"As they are always dissatisfied with the position which they occupy," he wrote, "and are always free to leave it, they think of nothing but the means of changing their fortunes, or increasing it. To minds thus predisposed, every new method which leads by a shorter road to wealth, every machine which spares labor, every instrument which diminishes the cost of production, every discovery which facilitates pleasures or augments them, seems to be the grandest effort of the human intellect."

The rich and powerful, like de Tocqueville, are satisfied with their lot and do not leave it. The promise of America is for the rest of us: we who dream of a better life. The inscription of the Statute of Liberty is the best evidence of this fact.

"Give me your tired, your poor, your huddled masses yearning to breathe free," the inscription reads, "The wretched refuse of your teeming shore. Send these, the homeless, tempest-tost to me. I lift my lamp beside the golden door."

The "golden door" Liberty refers to is the entrance to New York Harbor. The Statue of Liberty, a gift of friendship from the people of France commemorating the 100th anniversary of American independence, stands there welcoming all who come to that harbor. The sculptor, Auguste Bartholdi, said the Statue was intended to be "an immense and impressive symbol of human liberty." It was certainly that for the millions of immigrants who came to America during the last two centuries seeking freedom and the opportunity to make their dreams come true.

Four years after the Statue of Liberty was erected,

nearby Ellis Island was selected as the site of a much-needed "immigration depot" at a cost of $75,000. On the first day of operation, 2,251 people were inspected on Ellis Island. In the next six years, the number of hopeful new Americans increased to more than a million. Today, 60 percent of all Americans are descended from someone who came through Ellis Island.

In the 100 years between 1824 and 1924, 34 million immigrants from around the world landed on American soil. The first wave of immigrants were primarily Northern Europeans fleeing the starvation, oppression and social upheaval brought about by the Industrial Revolution. The second wave of immigrants streamed out of Southern and Eastern Europe. Most sought greater economic opportunities, but many were also the victims of religious persecution. It was said that the faces of a thousand nations were on board when the great steamships of the early twentieth century sailed into New York Harbor.

Like Columbus and the pilgrims and pioneers before them, each passenger on those ships sought the promise of America. The Old World lay behind them. Gone were the monarchies and kings, the systems of caste and peasantry, of famine and numbing poverty. Ahead was a New World, the promise of a new life and the opportunity to carve their own destiny.

Today, the United States is in the midst of another great wave of immigration that brings in roughly one million new residents a year. More than one in ten residents of the United States are immigrants, the highest share of the overall American population since the 1930s.

These figures don't include illegal immigrants, who are estimated to be arriving at the rate of 300,000 a year. The lure of a better life in the United States — in spite of the risks—has always been strong, but it was heightened by the economic boom of the 1990s. During that one decade, the number of illegal immigrants in the U.S. more than doubled.

People vote with their feet. For more than 500 years, people from all over the world have made their way to America. We have become, in the words of Israel Zangwill, "God's crucible," the great melting-pot where all the races are converging and reforming.

"This is the only country in the world which experiences this constant and repeated rebirth," Woodrow Wilson said. "Other countries depend upon the multiplication of their own native people. This country is constantly drinking strength out of new sources by the voluntary association with it of great bodies of strong men and forward-looking women out of other lands. And so by the gift of the free will of independent people it is being constantly renewed from generation to generation by the same process by which it was originally created. It is as if humanity had determined to see to it that this great nation, founded for the benefit of humanity, should not lack for the allegiance of the people of the world."

America is not a matter of birthplace, color or creed, or line of descent. America is a question of principle, purpose, character and hope.

"To every man his chance, to every man, regardless of his birth," Thomas Wolfe wrote, summing up the promise of America, "his shining golden opportunity. To every man the right to live, to work, to be himself, and to become whatever thing his manhood and his vision can contribute to make him."

The five stories that follow are vivid examples of the enduring nature of opportunity in America. Christopher Reeve has carried on a valiant battle—a battle he could only fight in America—to recover and be himself since his tragic accident, while Becky Simpson, called "the Mother Teresa of Appalachia," has carried on a one-woman crusade to provide opportunities for the poor in rural America.

Oprah Winfrey's journey from poverty to success and significance has provided inspiration to millions of Americans and countless others around the world. She stands as a shining example of an individual's ability to shape the nature of their lives by the choices they make and understanding that every gift we are given is given to us for a purpose.

Ben Carson's vision took him from being "the dumbest kid in his class" to the youngest individual to be named head of pediatric neurosurgery at John's Hopkins University. The perfection of his unique abilities has allowed him to do what no one had ever done before—separate Siamese twins joined at the head.

Chad Perlyn reminds us everyone has an opportunity to make a difference in this country. It doesn't matter who you are, where you are or how old you are. America is a willingness of the heart. We are limited only by the size of our dreams.

★ ★ ★ ★

Christopher Reeve

Christopher Reeve was at the height of his career when he was literally thrown from his horse. Overnight, the actor best known for his role as Superman, the man who can fly, found he could not walk. More than that, he found he could not speak, feed himself or sit without assistance.

After his injury, Chris was so dependent he could not safely be detached from a respirator for more than a few minutes at a time. Even breathing, the first and last test of life, had to be done for him. Now, with the help of a medical device called diaphragm pacing, he breathes on his own. Doctors said he would never move again. But he has. Chris is now able to move his arms and legs. More than ever, he is determined to reach the goal he announced to an astonished and disbelieving world shortly after his spinal cord was severed. He plans to walk again.

"I always have that picture in mind," he told CNN on January 1, 2004. "I live in the moment, dealing with day-to-day things. When I started diaphragm pacing, there was a moment of celebration, a moment of rejoicing. I had gotten something normal back. But then we went, OK, what's next? And that's the way it's been with all my movements."

Chris firmly believes his failure to live in the moment is what caused his accident. "I just didn't pay attention for a moment, that's all there is to it," he told Paula Zahn of CNN. "My horse and I were so mentally attuned, from all our time working together, that he knew my mind had gone away. I was thinking about a harder jump."

People often lose the present in the past and future. There is comfort in the security of the world we remember and hope in the world to come without the challenges of the present. But the cost of losing the present is the opportunities we forfeit. The next moment will bring another opportunity, but neither we nor the opportunity are the same. What we might have done, we can no longer do.

"You've got to be right here," Reeve says. "Whatever you are doing, you've got to fully focus, because you really pay a price if you don't."

Two years ago, Chris spoke candidly with a small group of people at a private reception in New York. "Maybe what happened to me was what had to happen to me to get my attention," he said. "I used to think nothing of taking a half million dollars for filming a thirty second commercial just to have money to fly my jet. But what happened changed me. Now I know the world can change in thirty seconds. I don't want to waste a minute."

As a result, Chris will tell you his understanding of what "the pursuit of happiness" means has changed. He says the most precious thing he has now is time with his wife and family. He has turned down tens of thousands of dollars just to see his son play hockey.

"All my life I had prided myself on being so self-sufficient," he says. "I didn't need anybody. And then I realized how lucky I am to have people who are there for me, no matter what. Yes, it may be an achievement to fly solo, but there is a great deal more true satisfaction in flying together."

Now, in addition to the grueling therapy required for his rehabilitation, Reeve carries on a hectic schedule designed to put a human face on spinal cord injury. As chairman of the Christopher Reeve Paralysis Foundation, he has raised millions of dollars for research, providing hope to the hopeless. For many of us, he seems to have gone from playing Superman to being superman.

"We all have a little voice inside us telling us whether we're

doing something decent or not," Chris says. "Something loving, something giving, something caring. But sometimes
there's a lot of chatter in our lives, and its hard to hear that little
voice. That's why I have to learn to be quiet sometimes and
listen. Having this disability has given me that opportunity."

"Life is pretty random," he concludes. "Anybody's life can
change in an instant. None of us are exempt. It's a question of
what we do afterwards that counts. How we find the meaning.
And once you see that as an opportunity rather than a complete disaster, then you can really get things done."

★ ★ ★ ★

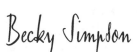

Becky Simpson remembers watching her little brother die of pneumonia when she was five years old. Two years later her sister almost followed him. The house was so cold, she recalls, it was warmer outside. She also remembers making, at that tender age, a promise that she would never, ever watch someone die without trying to help.

In 1962, her husband, Bobby, lost his sight and could no longer get work. Hard times got harder in rural Cranks Creek, Kentucky.

"We nearly starved to death," Bobby remembers. "What we had to live on was what we raised ourselves—garden stuff."

Ultimately, what saved them was an even bigger catastrophe. One summer, when it seemed things couldn't get much worse, the skies opened up. It rained seemingly without end for days, and their valley was hit with a series of floods. Soon there wasn't a bridge left in the county.

The damage done by the deluge was complicated by the ecological damage caused by strip mining in the mountains above them. The way Bobby remembers it, "There were maybe three good cars left in the whole valley. We lost all of our wells, and the water in our house was four feet deep."

But every problem presents an opportunity. Becky found hers.

She remembers standing on a crate near the bank of the river crying in frustration the third time her brother was flooded out. While she cried, the promise she had made so long ago came back to her and a new thought formed. What came to her was the knowledge that she had friends she hadn't met yet.

Becky got on the phone and got to work. She was determined to do whatever she could to solve this problem. She organized, cajoled and lobbied. She arranged meetings, put together petitions and testified at hearings. Before she was done, she had obtained $1 million to dredge the silt out of the local creek. Then she went to work looking for money for reclamation of the mountains. Surprising even herself, she was able to raise $940,000 to stabilize the mountains and restore the ecological base that had been destroyed by the strip mines.

"Human suffering has always moved me," Becky said, "But I had no idea that any one person could really do anything about it."

From that new understanding emerged the purpose and direction of her life. Though they lived on nothing more than Bobby's disability pay, the Simpsons founded the Cranks Creek Survival Center, which sees to those in need in a dozen counties in the tri-state area of Kentucky, Virginia and Tennessee.

Much of their effort goes to aid their neighbors—people like Franklin Hill, who was living in a coal shed until the Simpsons and their volunteers built him a little twelve-foot by twenty four-foot house; Henry Furman, who lived by himself in a pump house; and Michael Taylor, who lived in a floorless chicken coop with his fourteen-month-old baby.

In all, the Simpsons have restored more than 800 houses in the surrounding hills. Thousands of volunteers—Becky's unknown friends—have come to help. They have come from the entire east coast and more than a dozen foreign nations, including India, China, Africa and Brazil. It is a testimony to the depth of poverty in Appalachia that residents of countries we tend to think of as poor would travel halfway around the world to aid Americans who are even poorer.

Bobby supervises the building projects and directs the gathering of supplies. Though sightless, he has learned the highways by heart, navigating his driver with a collection of audio and visual cues he has stored in his mind. "A lot of handicapped people just sit down and don't try to do nothing," he explains, "but there is always something you can do if you try." While decent housing is the greatest need, the Simpsons also provide clothing, food and financial assistance. Bobby says it follows the seasons. "Beginning the first of the year, people come by to get garden seeds, fertilizer and stuff. Then school starts, and people are hunting for school clothing, shoes and sweaters. Gets fall and everybody starts hunting something to stay warm. Then it's Thanksgiving time."

At Thanksgiving, the Simpsons provide dinner for over 400 families. Christmas is a repeat performance on a larger scale. On average they feed 700 people every Christmas—most of them coal miners who have been laid off and are out of work.

"Whatever someone needs, we try to do," Becky says. "It's like a little miracle. It pleases me to death to be able to help someone else. I had a dream since I was a child that someday I was going to help needy people, and now I can do it. If I hear of somebody out of food, I can take them food. Most of the time, I can find them pretty good clothing in here, bed clothes, whatever they need. It has to be a miracle. That's the only way I can explain it."

"If we hadn't started doing this, I'd be dead and gone," Bobby adds. "There's too many people out there that needs help. I just couldn't give up. If you can love people good enough, you kind of forget yourself and your problems in helping them."

"Somebody once said it was my work," Becky concludes. "I said, no, it ain't my work. It's my life."

★ ★ ★ ★

Ben Carson

When he was thirty-three years old, Ben Carson was named director of pediatric neurosurgery at Johns Hopkins University Hospital in Baltimore, Maryland. He is the youngest person to ever hold that position. Not bad for someone who used to be called "the dumbest kid in the fifth grade."

Ben Carson's mother, Sonya, was born into a large and extremely poor family in rural Tennessee. She had twenty-three brothers and sisters. Her family was so poor that Sonya spent most of her childhood in foster homes. When Ben's father came along, proposed marriage and promised her a good life up north in Detroit, Michigan, Sonya was quick to agree—even though she was only thirteen years old.

At first everything went well, but when Ben was eight years old he became aware that something was dreadfully wrong with his family. The first thing he noticed was the sound of silence. His father and mother simply stopped talking to each other. Then his father's business trips seem to come more often and last longer. Finally, his mother announced his father would not be living with them any more. She said she had found out he was a bigamist. He had a wife and another family in another town, and she had asked him to leave.

When Ben's father left, he took all of the family's income with him. His mother had no job skills or work experience, but she was determined to take care of her family—and she did, taking a job cleaning houses. She was equally determined her boys would amount to something.

"The most important gift my mother gave me," Ben has said "was the sense of self-determination. She made it clear that the person who had the most to do with what happened to you was you."

When Sonya heard Ben was being called a dummy and failing most of his subjects in school, she laid down the law. She told him they were going to turn off the television—with the exception of two shows a week—and start reading. She said she expected him to read at least two books a week and write a book report for her describing what he had read. He didn't know it at the time, but his mother had found the key that would unlock his future and someday enable his dreams to come true.

Ben began reading whenever and wherever he could. He read before school and after school. He even read books when he was waiting for the bus to go to school. Two years later, he had gone from "the dumbest kid in the fifth grade" to the top of his class. He graduated from Wilson High School third in his class and won a scholarship to Yale University.

Carson went on to the University of Michigan School of Medicine. While he was there, he worked odd jobs during the summer to help pay his way. He worked on an assembly line for Chrysler Motor Company, supervised a highway trash collection crew and operated a crane for a steel company.

Strangely, operating this heavy equipment prepared him for the delicate tasks he would soon undertake. As he moved the large pieces of steel into position, he realized he had an unusual ability to think and see in three dimensions, a gift that would later prove invaluable as a surgeon, enabling him to understand what was happening even in parts of the brain he could not actually see.

With this insight into his unique abilities, Carson applied to do his residency at Johns Hopkins University, specializing in neurosurgery. A year after completing his residency, he joined the faculty at Johns Hopkins and, only a few months later, was asked to fill the position of chief of pediatric neurosurgery.

Shortly thereafter, Ben Carson met Miranda Francisco.

Miranda was having as many as 100 seizures a day. Other doctors had given her no hope of recovery. She had almost stopped eating. She was forgetting how to walk and talk and needed constant supervision.

Carson noticed the seizures almost always began on her right side, causing him to think the problem lay somewhere in the left side of her brain. The only procedure he could identify that might help was a hemispherectomy, which involves removing one side, or half, of her brain. The procedure had only been attempted a few times with little success, but it appeared to be the only alternative to simply watching the girl die.

Ben had to operate slowly and meticulously because Miranda's brain had been so damaged by the seizures that the slightest touch caused the tissue to bleed. Finally, ten hours after he began, he had succeeded in removing half the girl's brain.

Still, no one knew what that meant. Had they cured the problem? Would she live? Would she be able to walk and talk, or would she be paralyzed on the right side of the body? No one knew. As they were wheeling her out of surgery, Miranda's mother leaned over and kissed her daughter. Miranda's eyes opened slightly. In a small voice she said, "I love you, Mommy and Daddy," and the questions were answered.

Miranda made a full recovery and became the first of many hemispherectomies Carson would perform. Building on this experience, he later became the first surgeon to successfully separate Siamese twins joined at the head.

Now, whenever he talks to young people, Carson introduces himself as the director of pediatric neurosurgery at Johns Hopkins University and a former "class dummy."

"Everybody has obstacles," he says, "but success will be determined by how we relate to those obstacles. The obstacle can be a containing fence, or it can simply be a hurdle that strengthens you for the next barrier."

★ ★ ★ ★

Oprah Winfrey has left an indelible mark on our society. Born at home in rural Mississippi to unwed parents, she has become one of the most important figures in popular American culture, entering 20 million homes every day, touching and transforming thousands of lives. She is the first African-American woman billionaire, the only woman to own and produce her own talk show, and the most honored person in broadcasting. Few have risen so far, so fast.

Some call her lucky, but Oprah doesn't believe in luck. She believes "luck is preparation meeting opportunity."

Oprah was born in Kosciusko, Mississippi, on January 29, 1954. Her mother was an eighteen-year-old housemaid named Vernita Lee. Her father, Vernon Winfrey, was a twenty-year-old soldier stationed nearby.

For the first six years of her life, Oprah lived on a farm with her grandmother. Even then, she knew her life would be different than those around her. She distinctly remembers standing on the back porch when she was four watching her grandmother struggling to do the laundry by hand and thinking, "My life won't be like this. It will be better."

Oprah's grandmother gave her the foundation for success, teaching her to read when most children were still learning to speak. By the time she was three, she was reciting speeches in church, repeating sermons and poems she had memorized. By the time she was six, she had spoken at nearly every church in Nashville.

"Whatever you do a lot of, you get good at doing," Oprah

says. "That's how this whole broadcasting career started for me. I was known for talking."

When she was six, Oprah went to live with her mother in Milwaukee. Though she didn't recognize it at the time, they were living in poverty. Three years later, when she was nine, she was raped by a cousin. She was later sexually molested by an uncle and then a friend of the family.

In her hurt and anger, Oprah rebelled. She became a sexually promiscuous teenager and got into a lot of trouble. By the time she was thirteen, she was so out of control that her mother sent her to a juvenile detention home. Fortunately for her, all the beds were filled, and she was denied admission. As an alternative, she was sent to Nashville to live with her father. She was pregnant when she arrived and gave birth to a stillborn baby boy shortly thereafter.

The death of her baby devastated her. Even at the tender age of fourteen, Oprah knew that if her life was in fact going to be better than those of her mother and grandmother she had to turn herself around. Her father reinforced her commitment with strict rules and discipline. He made sure she stuck to a midnight curfew, and he required her to read one book and complete a book report each week. He encouraged her to do her best and maintain good grades in school.

Three years later, Oprah Winfrey was hired by WVOL radio in Nashville. Two years later, at the age of nineteen, she was hired by WTVF-TV. She became the youngest person, and the first African-American woman, to anchor the news in Nashville.

In 1976, when she was twenty-two years old, Oprah moved to Baltimore to join WJZ-TV as co-anchor of the six o'clock news. She soon was given the additional responsibility of co-hosting the station's local talk show, *People Are Talking*. The quality of her work in Baltimore drew the attention of network executives in Chicago, who recruited her to host a faltering talk show called *AM Chicago*. In less than a year, Oprah turned *AM Chicago* into the hottest show in town. The format was soon expanded to one hour and, in September 1985, renamed *The Oprah Winfrey Show*. *The Oprah Winfrey Show* went national in 1986. A year later, it became the number one talk show in national syndication. The following year, the program received three Daytime Emmy Awards, the first of many honors to follow.

"Our original goal was to uplift, enlighten, encourage and entertain through the medium of television," Oprah says. Now with her great success has come a broader mission: "To use television to transform people's lives, to make viewers see themselves differently and bring happiness and a sense of fulfillment into every home."

Oprah and *The Oprah Winfrey Show* have now received a total of thirty-eight Daytime Emmy Awards. She received both an Academy Award and Golden Globe nomination for her performance in *The Color Purple* and produced a series of award-winning films and television specials, including *Tuesdays With Morrie*, which received four Emmy Awards in September 2000.

But the greatest tribute to her success is the use she has made of that success. Oprah knows every gift we are given is given to us for a purpose. She has seized every opportunity to use the gifts she has been given to give back.

As Barbara Walters said, "The only thing greater than Oprah's accomplishments is the size of her heart."

Through The Angel Network and her private foundation, Oprah has provided millions of dollars and been the catalyst for thousands of grants to charities that are making a difference for children in need. As one small example of her impact, in 2002, Oprah organized an initiative she called ChristmasKindness in South Africa. As part of this effort, Oprah and her team of volunteers brought gifts and Christmas joy to 50,000 South African children.

"When I was twelve and on welfare with my mother, I was

told we weren't going to have a Christmas," she explains. "Some nuns showed up at the last minute and brought food and presents. I never forgot that. I wanted to create something like that for these children."

For all her success, Oprah has not forgotten where she came from. "I understand what it means to be poor and not have your possibilities revealed to you," she has said. "But I also believe that you tend to create your own blessings. You have to prepare yourself so that when opportunity comes you're ready."

★ ★ ★ ★

Chad Perlyn

When he was a sophomore at Pine Crest High School in
Florida, Chad Perlyn managed to do something his county
government had been unable to do: He found a way to provide
quality health care at no cost for more than 100 foster children
in the Broward County area.

The idea came to him after he was selected to enter the
Enterprise Ambassador Program at the Fried Business School.
The focus of this program was on how to create and run a
business, but as part of their training, students were asked to
raise money for a community service project.

Chad organized a triathlon as a fund-raising event. Every
participant had to compete in a trike-a-thon, rocking chair race
and a walk-a-thon with the proceeds going to charity. To
everyone's surprise, the event raised over $7,000.

Chad donated the money to shelter for abused children in
Broward County. At the same time, buoyed by the
triathlon's success, he initiated a toy drive for the Children's
Home Society, which places kids from abusive or under-
privileged families in foster homes.

That's when Chad got the inspiration for the program he
called DOC-ADOPT. "The idea for DOC-ADOPT clicked
when I visited some of the kids from the Children's Home
Society. One girl had been punched in the mouth by her dad.
She had lost some of her teeth as a result but couldn't get them
fixed because none of the clinics would do that kind of work."

Chad decided to pair kids with doctors and dentists
who could be persuaded to provide a year's free medical services for a child in need. Within a year, 120 doctors were

participating in the program. Many were so impressed with Chad and DOC-ADOPT they offered to extend their services for several years and adopt more than one child. Before he graduated from high school, Chad had received the formal endorsement of the Broward County Health and Rehabilitation Services, Broward Dental Association and Broward Medical Association. The program continued under their auspices when Chad went on to college.

In the opportunity he was given to help others, Chad found himself. Largely as a result of his experience with DOC-ADOPT he decided to attend the University of Miami School of Medicine. He went on to do his residency in St. Louis and is currently at Oxford University, working on his Ph.D. in molecular biology. Chad plans to spend three years doing research in craniofacial abnormalities and then return to St. Louis to complete his training as a pediatric plastic surgeon.

"There are so many kids who are deprived of so much," he says. "Anything we can do to make their lives better is worth doing. That's who I am. That's where I want to be."

Three

RESPONSIBILITY

★ ★ ★ ★

Liberty means responsibility.

George Bernard Shaw

hat America needs," Viktor Frankl once said, "is a Statue of Responsibility." Frankl, author of the best-selling book *Man's Search for Meaning,* suggested we put it on the west coast for balance.

Responsibility is often associated with blame and burden. It should more accurately be associated with opportunity and action.

"Response," after all, is at the root of the word. Ten percent of life has to do with what happens to us. The other ninety percent is shaped by how we respond. It is the way we change the world, the catalytic factor driving the choices that define who we are and what our country will become.

"Response ability" is the essence of a free man's life. We are free to the degree we accept responsibility; we lose freedom and liberty to the degree we abdicate our responsibility or let others act for us.

The preamble to the Constitution of the United States reflects this fundamental fact. "We the people of the United States" the preamble begins. It is a proud declaration of power and a claim of responsibility. We are the architects of our government. We determine the nature of our society. Implicit in this is the understanding that if we do not create a society close to our heart's desire, someone else will—and their desire may be far from our own.

When Alexis de Tocqueville arrived in the United States, the power of a free people was already evident. As an aristocrat and the son of an aristocratic state, he had never seen anything like it.

"These Americans are peculiar people," he said. "If, in a local community, a citizen becomes aware of a human need which is not being met, he thereupon discusses the situation with his neighbors. Suddenly, a committee comes into existence. The committee begins to operate on behalf of the need, and a new community function is established."

Contrary to European societies, de Tocqueville noted, citizens of the United States are taught from infancy to rely upon their own exertions and claim assistance only when they are unable to do without it. This was something new to the world.

In America, power resides with the people. It is delegated up not down. As President Dwight D. Eisenhower observed, "The true slogan of a democracy is not 'Let the government do it,'" he said, "'but rather 'Let's do it ourselves.' This is the spirit of a people dedicated to helping themselves—and one another."

That same spirit is abundantly evident in America today. Americans routinely come together to build churches and schools and address community problems. One of the clearest examples is the nonprofit world, which embodies responsibility.

The only reason nonprofit organizations exist is to save or change lives. While even the purest purpose can be perverted by those seeking some personal advantage, by and large charities are organized and operated by individual citizens banded together—much as de Tocqueville observed some 200 years ago—to address common concerns and solve social and political problems.

According to the Internal Revenue Service, which tracks nonprofits for tax purposes, there are over 1 million nonprofit organizations in the United States. Fifty thousand new organizations are formed every year. In addition, there are tens of thousands of trade and advocacy groups organized by individual citizens to speak to issues of common concern. In Washington, D.C., where I work, it is hard to escape them. They are abundantly present.

Though I have been in Washington most of my adult life, I have never ceased to be amazed at the number of these groups, their range and specificity of their interests. There is an association focused on any issue you can imagine and any cause for concern.

Responsibility follows power. In the end, we are responsible not only for our own actions, but the actions of those who work for us, including our civic and political leaders. President Reagan went so far as to say his primary job was to simply unmask the power of the American people.

President Reagan's observation reflects his understanding of the primacy of the people in democracy. A quarter of a century before, President John F. Kennedy spoke to the same theme.

"And so, my fellow Americans," President Kennedy said as he concluded his inaugural address, "ask not what your country can do for you—ask what you can do for your country."

While the role of the individual in the private sector is less visible, it is equally important. Here, farsighted leaders often correlate responsibility with the best use of power.

"As the duty is precisely corresponded to power," John Randolph said, "it follows that the richer, the wiser, the more powerful a man is, the greater is the obligation upon him to employ his gifts in lessening the sum of human misery."

Every right carries a responsibility; every gift, an obligation; every opportunity, a duty. One captain of industry who well understood this was Peter Grace, grandson of the founder of W. R. Grace. Peter had taken the helm of the billion-dollar company while still in his thirties. When I met him in 1988, he was nearly ninety and carried the scars of some fifty years on the public stage.

Grace had been lionized and vilified, praised for his visionary leadership and denounced for his aggressive business tactics. Respected, loved and feared by his peers, few in corporate America had as much power.

When I asked him to tell me the greatest lesson in his life, he began to talk about responsibility. Peter said that as a boy he was tutored by Father James Keller, founder of The Christophers.

"Whenever I came to him to describe some great horror I had heard about or some injustice in the world, Father Keller's response was always the same," Peter said. "As I finished describing whatever caused my concern, he would say, 'Well, what are you going to do about it?'"

Though it was not commonly known, Grace was responsible for an enormous body of good works that spoke eloquently to his own sense of responsibility. It was his answer to Keller's charge. He supported health clinics in South America, worked to find a cure for leprosy, helped build homes for Mother Teresa and provided aid to those in need around the world through the Knights of Malta.

Ultimately, as his story suggests, it comes down to us. When we exercise our "response ability," we change the world around us. As Robert Kennedy observed, few of us will have the greatness to bend history itself, but each of us can do something.

"Each time a man stands up for an ideal," Kennedy said, "or acts to improve the lot others, or strikes out against injustice, he sends forth a tiny ripple of hope." Day by day, we change the world with everything we do or do not do. The five people who follow have done more than most and provided more than a ripple of hope.

Azim Khamisa's response to the murder of his son tests the boundaries of faith and forgiveness. His ability to answer hate with love provides an example of courage and commitment to the ideal of justice that few can match.

Bea Gaddy went from eating out of garbage cans to feeding hundreds of people a day and 25,000 people every year in the nation's largest Thanksgiving Day dinner, while Ranya Kelly, Kent Amos and Emily Kumpel were confronted by other challenges. Their responses to the specific questions they were asked demonstrate how our lives are shaped by the choices we make and the way God works through us to change the world.

Together, these people speak to the uniqueness of our ability to respond to the opportunities before us. In the words of Martin Luther King, Jr., "Every person must feel responsibility to discover his mission in life. God has given each normal person a capacity to achieve some end."

In America, everyone can contribute. Everyone is needed. For our country to be as great as it can be, everyone must take responsibility.

★ ★ ★ ★

After living without heat and light for two months and being unable to feed her children, Bea Gaddy was forced to her knees.

"I asked the Supreme Being to show me how to take care of my children. I did not ask for anybody else's children," she said candidly. "I just wanted to know how to feed my children and myself."

Bea had been homeless most of her life. Her strongest memory is of hunger. "As a child we used to fight at the garbage cans," she recalls. "We all did it—my brothers and myself. Other families around us.

"It is degrading. It is very dehumanizing. But you don't think about that if you're a child and you're hungry. You go into that can and get that food, wash it off and use it. You don't think about it, because not a soul is saying, 'Why you in that can? Let me show you a better way.' You've got to find your own way to come out of that can."

As an adult most of Bea's time was spent sitting and "waiting for a welfare check." In the early sixties, after she was evicted from her apartment in Brooklyn, she moved to Baltimore to be near a friend. "I was living in Patterson Park. I was getting food stamps," she remembers, "but I still couldn't feed my children or pay the rent."

The prayer Bea made came out of her desperation, but with it she sent a promise.

"Show me how to do these things and I promise I will forever give back," she said. "I will walk with the people. I will do whatever I have to do to make people stop sitting and feeling sorry for themselves."

Shortly after her prayer, Bea had a flash of inspiration. She went down to her church and asked her pastor if she could borrow a garbage can that had wheels. While her neighbors watched through drawn curtains, she wheeled it up to the corner market.

Somehow she found the courage to ask the owner, "Would you please give me the food that you are going to throw away tonight?"

The man looked at her strangely, Bea remembers. "I thought the man was going to say, 'Get out of my store,' but he didn't. He asked me why I wanted it, and when I said, 'So we can eat it,' he practically filled this huge can up before I came out of the store."

At a second store, the owner finished filling the can. Encouraged by her success, Bea emptied the can at home and went to a third store down the street.

"This man actually filled up the whole garbage can with food," Bea remembers. "When I came home this time, everybody came out on the street, and I said there's no stopping us now."

Though she started out thinking only of herself, she soon realized she had an opportunity to do so much more. She came up with the idea of opening an emergency food center. When that succeeded, she moved from food to shelter, sleeping in the basement of her own home to make room for others upstairs. Then she broadened her focus to other opportunities to help people in need.

"If people need a place to stay and they are not a threat to themselves or anyone else, I will make space for them," she told me. "I beg for food, houses and clothes. I have even begged for money to bury people. I have to. I made a promise and I love it. I need everybody I'm helping as much as they need me."

Bea's greatest satisfaction was the Thanksgiving Day dinner she organized every year until she died in 2002. It grew to become the nation's largest Thanksgiving Day dinner, annually feeding as many as 25,000 people who had nowhere else to go.

When she looked back at it, Bea said the hardest part was learning to believe in herself.

"If you don't have self-worth, if you don't have respect for yourself, how can you respect anyone else?" she says. "I had to learn that I had a brain, because I had been told I was no good and never going to amount to anything. Then I had to learn to use it.

"I figured that out when I knew I could no longer sit and wait for someone to bring me food. I could no longer sit and wait until they bring me some underwear for my children and myself. Once I knew I could do it, I wondered why, in the name of God, I sat waiting all those years. In this country, the sky's the limit."

★ ★ ★ ★

On January 21, 1995, a twenty-year-old San Diego University Student, Tariq Khamisa, was shot and killed while delivering pizzas. His assailant was a fourteen-year-old boy named Tony Hicks. Tony and three other gang members surrounded Tariq and demanded his money. When Tariq refused, the eighteen-year-old gang leader ordered Tony to fire the fatal bullet.

Tony admitted the crime and pled guilty to first degree murder in April 1996. He was the first juvenile in the state of California to be tried as an adult under a new law that went into effect just three weeks before his crime.

At sentencing, Tony delivered an emotional and remorseful speech, accepting responsibility for his actions and asking for the family's forgiveness. He was sentenced to a prison term of twenty-five years at New Folsom California State Prison in Sacramento and will not be eligible for parole until 2017.

While Tony Hicks's ability to accept responsibility for his actions may have been expected, Azim Khamisa's response when he learned of his son's murder was not. Instead of demanding revenge and retribution, he reached out in forgiveness to Tony's family.

"From the onset," he says, "I saw victims on both ends of the gun. Two of America's sons were lost—one forever and one to the state prison system."

Azim's strength came from his Ismaili Muslim faith, his family roots and his determination to honor his son in a meaningful way. In the Ismaili Muslim faith, special prayers are recited for the departed soul of a loved one at the funeral and then ten days, forty days, six months, a year later and every year thereafter. During the forty-day prayers, one of Azim's spiritual teachers gave him the answer he had been searching for and a way to transform his loss.

"After passing from this world," the teacher said, "the soul remains in close proximity to the family and loved ones during the forty days of grieving. After forty days, the soul moves to a new level of consciousness. Grieving past this time impedes the soul's journey. Compassionate acts undertaken in the name of the departed are 'spiritual currency' that will transfer Tariq's soul and help speed his journey."

While it is human to grieve, Azim realized he had to break the paralysis of grief and find a good deed to do in Tariq's name. "I knew Tariq was at peace, even though I was not. I began to understand that to find peace for myself, I needed to find something that I could do for Tariq."

Then came the inspiration. "What if I became a foe—not of the boy who killed my son—but of the forces which led him to kill my son?" Azim wondered.

With that embryonic thought the Tariq Khamisa Foundation was born. Azim, an international businessman, started talking to everyone he knew about his concept for the Foundation and found the response incredible. The Khamisa Foundation is dedicated to creating safer communities by cultivating personal responsibility and guiding young people away from gangs and violence.

In the same spirit, Khamisa told the San Diego prosecutor he wanted to meet Ples Felix, the grandfather and guardian of Tariq's killer, to see if he would considering joining the battle to end youth violence. On November 3, 1995, the father of the boy who had been killed met the grandfather of the boy who had killed him.

"We both carry a burden of loss," Azim told Tony's grandfather. "Help me carry mine. Let me help you carry yours."

The two men found they shared more than loss. They

shared a strong faith and a burning desire to end the plague of youth violence in our country.

Felix, a manager for the city of San Diego, was quick to join the advisory board of the Khamisa Foundation. Today, Ples and Azim frequently stand together at schools and conferences talking about the burden they share and the way youth violence had impacted their families. In the eight years since the Foundation was created, they have reached more than 350,000 kids.

"Most of these kids can be saved," Azim says. "We lose a child to a gun every ninety-two minutes in the United States. Our society has come to accept these killings as normal. When did we decide this was normal?"

Homicide and suicide rates are higher in the United States than in any of the twenty-six wealthiest nations in the world, he notes. In fact, the homicide rate for young males in the United States is ten times higher than in Canada and twenty-eight times higher than it is in France and Germany.

"Education is the key," Azim says. "We teach academic subjects, and we assume life skills will somehow be acquired along the way. Not a safe assumption! The curriculum has to include things like communication, conflict resolution, parenting, family dynamics, critical thinking, values and ethics."

In April 2000, five years after Tariq's death, Azim Khamisa and Tony Hicks met for the first time, face to face, at Folsom Prison. One seeking forgiveness, the other giving it. The two men embraced and cried.

★ ★ ★ ★

Ranya Kelly

Fifteen years ago, Ranya Kelly, a housewife living in a suburb of Denver, looked in a dumpster behind a mall and got a surprise.

"I was looking for a box to do some Christmas shipping and I found 500 pairs of shoes," she says. "I couldn't believe what I saw."

Later that evening, Ranya came back with her husband and picked all the shoes out of the trash. She took them home and spread them out on the floor. After sorting through them, she began giving them away to her friends and family.

But she soon found she had many more than she could possibly give away. Her bonanza had become a burden. Unable to live with the thought that these perfectly good shoes would go to waste, Ranya decided to take the rest to a local shelter.

"I never knew about the shelters or people in need," Ranya said. "I grew up in an upper-middle class family. I was never involved with people. I was just trying to think of somewhere I could drop these shoes off so they wouldn't go to waste."

What she saw at the shelter changed her life.

"There was a woman standing in the doorway," Ranya remembers, "her pants dragging on the floor. She had a little baby about two or three with her. She was pregnant and barefoot in the middle of January. I couldn't believe it. The look in her eye and her gratitude changed my life."

In the eleven years since that look of gratitude, the "Shoe Lady," as Ranya is now known, has managed to find and distribute more than $15 million worth of shoes and other merchandise to people in need. She operates out of her suburban

Colorado home on a budget of less than $15,000 a year.
Ranya no longer scours dumpsters, favoring a direct
approach through the front door of retailers and manufactur-
ers, but her message hasn't changed. She serves as a liaison
between those who need help and those who can provide it.

"We all have this need to be needed," Ranya says. "If we are
not responsible for something, we are lost. But to be responsible just for yourself is a waste of time. The more I got involved
with people, the more I felt needed and the happier I became."

★ ★ ★ ★

Fifteen years ago, Kent Amos's son came home from school with some new friends. "The boys were OK," Kent said, "but they weren't the kind of kids I thought my son should associate with." The kids were rude and poorly spoken. They had little interest in anything other than sports. Kent's first thought was that these kids would drag his son down. He thought about forbidding his son to associate with such a rough crowd. Then he had a second thought—why not lift the others up?

"We embraced those children," he says. "We said if they were going to be *in* this house, they are going to be *of* this house. If they are going to be around this house, this house is going to be their home. If you care for your child, how could you not care for his friends?"

With that, Kent and his wife, Carmen, embarked on an effort to provide African American teenagers in the District of Columbia with a loving, caring and disciplined environment. They opened their home and wallet to an extended family that now numbers more than 100. They provided an atmosphere free of hopelessness and crime and full of encouragement, guidance and love.

At first, the Amos "family" met four nights a week, and to hear him describe it, Kent simply did what any good parent would do. He talked with them, checked their report cards, provided advice and encouraged them to do their best.

Now as many as twenty-five kids a night meet in the Amos home. The teenagers enjoy a family dinner and two hours of learning without TV or radio. And their education doesn't stop with their homework. They learn something about life, values and themselves.

Kent has guided nineteen of his kids through high school and college. Eighteen more are currently in college. Kent is paying the tuition for four of them and helping the rest. All in all, he has invested more than half a million dollars in his extended family.

Kent Amos firmly believes that the source of most of the difficulties these children face is that they have not been taught the values necessary to withstand temptation and stay out of trouble. "You keep hearing that we may be the first generation that will not give to the next generation more than was given to us. But the biggest problem with that statement is the people who say that are measuring things, not values. We seem to be more worried about giving children that which we didn't have than we are about giving them what we were given."

"My children have the ultimate decision on almost everything they do," he says, "starting at a very young age. All I am doing is trying to get them to internalize a set of values. They need to know there are things of value, but values transcend things."

Kent does what he does because he considers himself fortunate. Although he was blessed with a more privileged upbringing than most of his contemporaries and was surrounded by a positive and supportive family, he remembers flirting with crime and the temptations provided by many of his peers. He never excelled academically, and it was not until after a seven-year stint in the U.S. Army that he completed college.

"I learned it is never too late to turn your life around or too early to start," he says.

Kent spent fifteen years with the Xerox Corporation, working his way up through a series of sales and management positions. After his retirement from Xerox, he worked with a consulting group until he resigned his position to spend all of his time working with kids.

"You have to ask yourself what is your legacy?" Kent says. "No one rises alone. There are always those who contribute to your well-being. I am a product not only of today but yesterday. Battles were fought for the way of life I enjoy, and it is my responsibility to see that way of life continues."

★ ★ ★ ★

Emily Kumpel

The first time I called Emily Kumpel, I was somewhat taken aback. I was told the eleven-year old couldn't come to the phone because she was interviewing Desmond Tutu.

I probably shouldn't have been surprised. Emily filled a school library in South Africa with books at the age of seven, started a service program for kids at the age of eight, and by nine had her own radio program. Emily's program involved working as a volunteer reporter for the Peabody Award-winning radio show *Kid Company*. This weekly two-hour show provides a forum for children to express their own views. Emily was given responsibility for the radio's global correspondence.

"Even at that age, she was an incredible reporter with an innate capacity to understand world events," Rachel Burg, the show's programming director says. "She feels she has a moral responsibility to the public, and she has an insatiable drive to help kids understand what's going on and what they can do about it."

Emily's book project is a good example. In the course of researching apartheid in South Africa, Emily read an article about Dr. Wayne Dudley, a professor at Salem State College, who had gathered a shipment of books and sent them to South African high school students after Nelson Mandela was sworn in as president.

Emily was so fascinated by this project she contacted Dr. Dudley and offered to help. She said she thought it was important to provide books for younger children as well, volunteering to provide one elementary school in South Africa with all the reference, reading and text books it would need.

To do this, Emily organized book drives at her school, wrote a letter to the editor of the local paper encouraging people to donate their books, and placed posters and boxes around town encouraging participation in her book drive. She also organized bake sales to raise money to send the books to South Africa.

When her letter to the editor spurred community interest, Emily was asked to make presentations to a number of different civic groups. She challenged them to match any profit that her fund-raisers produced.

In 1994, the book drive's first year, Emily sent thirty boxes of books to the needy children in South Africa. The following year, she collected over 100 boxes for a total of 4,000 books. By August she had another 1,000 books collected for a December shipment. Ten years later, Emily, along with other organizations that joined her in this effort, has collected and sent 2.3 million books to South Africa.

"Some people ask me why I do this," Emily says. "I find it impossible not to. With every service experience since the book drive, I have found the same thing. I read about the problem, think about something concrete to do, and simply believe that it is my responsibility to do it. If I do nothing, the problem will still be there. It is up to me to work out a solution."

Emily found many other opportunities to be of service before going off to Johns Hopkins University to study mechanical engineering. After school, she plans to join the Peace Corps or work with Engineers Without Frontiers on projects related to sustainable development.

"I think it is easy for young people to sit back and believe that the world and its affairs belong to the politicians, rock stars and CEOs, and that ordinary citizens—including young people—are not responsible for the good or bad things that happen," Emily says. "There are some things in the world not in our control, but there is so much that is. Every young person is just as responsible as politicians or teachers or other adults for trying to make a positive change in the world.

"A common phrase heard by young people is that 'Youth are the future.' That's not entirely true. We are the future, but more importantly, we are here now. We have just as much capacity for love, responsibility and goodness as anyone else in the world. It is up to us to make sure we begin making change."

Four

EQUALITY

★ ★ ★ ★

We hold these truths be self-evident, that all men are created equal.

The Declaration of Independence

Equality is the keystone of democracy. From it flow liberty, opportunity and responsibility.

"We hold these truths to be sacred and undeniable," Thomas Jefferson wrote in the original draft of Declaration of Independence, "that all men are created equal and independent, that *from that equal creation they derive rights inherent and inalienable,* among which are the preservation of life, and liberty, and the pursuit of happiness."

The printer and publisher Benjamin Franklin perfected Jefferson's prose and gave the Continental Congress the language familiar to us today. A simple statement. Five words: All men are created equal.

It can be argued that no other concept has had such a profound impact on American society. No single phrase is closer to the heart of America or more institutionalized and broadly accepted in principle; yet, none of our founding principles has been the source of more controversy or more frequently challenged in application.

When the Declaration of Independence was written, the total population of what would soon become the United States of America was about 2.3 million. About 460,000 of these people were slaves and therefore excluded from the equal protection of the law.

As he signed the document he had written, Jefferson said, perhaps with a sense of foreboding for what would inevitably come as a consequence of this duplicity, "I tremble for my country when I consider God is just."

Still, for an aristocrat like Alexis de Tocqueville, the difference between what he saw in America and what he was used to seeing abroad was striking.

"The more I advanced in the study of American society," he said, "the more I perceived that this equality of condition is the fundamental fact from which all others seem to be derived, and the central point at which all my observations constantly terminated." He went on to say that nothing he saw in the United States struck him more forcibly than the general equality of conditions among the people.

The equality de Tocqueville saw was not simply a question of material condition. It was also a frame of mind and a question of attitude. To a man of his birth, it was amazing to see a society where every citizen saw himself the equal of every other citizen and inferior to no one.

"Every citizen has an equal share of power, and participates equally in the government of the state," he wrote in describing this novel situation. And as a consequence, "Every individual is always supposed to be as well informed, as virtuous and as strong as any of his fellow-citizens."

But it wasn't long before the reality of equality in America began to be challenged. African-Americans fought for full inclusion, using Jefferson's language to challenge slavery. The ideal of equality led Northern states to free slaves within their borders in the 1780s, 1790s and early in the 1800s. Abolitionists used the same ideal to attack slavery in the South before the Civil War. They found a powerful voice in a former slave named Frederick Douglass.

Douglass was born in 1818 in Tuckahoe, Maryland. At the age of nine, he was sent to work as a houseboy in Baltimore. His mistress there taught her own son, Tommy, to read and occasionally would teach Douglass, even though it was unlawful at that time to teach slaves to read and write.

Douglass's lessons stopped when the master of the house caught wind of what was going on and informed his wife of the consequences of her actions. When a black man learned to read, he warned, there was no con- trolling him. The lesson was not lost on Douglass. Learning became his passion. Surreptitiously, he copied Tommy's schoolwork, retracing the letters in his own hand. He learned to decipher letters on street signs, stores and sailing boats. He bribed white children he met on the streets, trading bread and cookies for words.

Douglass was filled with "a determination to learn to read at any cost." Though he was closely watched and constantly suspected of having a book, these efforts aimed at control were too late. By the time he was thir- teen, he had succeeded.

"The first never-to-be-retraced step had been taken," he said. "Teaching me the alphabet had been the inch given, and I was now only waiting the opportunity to take the mile."

When he was twenty, his master's prediction came true. Douglass escaped to New York City and then fled across the sea to England, where he stayed until friends purchased his freedom. In the meantime, he earned a reputation as a powerful orator, author and publisher.

Shortly after his return to the United States, Douglass was asked to give an address in New York on Independence Day. He accepted, calling his speech "If I had a Country, I Should be a Patriot."

"I can read with pleasure your Constitution to

establish justice and secure the blessings of liberty to posterity. Those are precious sayings to my mind," Douglass said. "But when I remember that the blood of four sisters and one brother is making fat the soil of Maryland and Virginia — when I remember that my aged grandmother . . . reared twelve children for the Southern slave market, and these one after another . . . were torn from her bosom — when I remember that when she became too much racked for toil, she was turned out by a professed Christian master to grope her way in the darkness of old age, literally to die with none to help her, and the institutions of this country sanctioning and sanctifying this crime, I have no words of eulogy, I have no patriotism. . . . No, I make no pretension of patriotism. So long as my voice can be heard on this or the other side of the Atlantic, I will hold up America to the lightening scorn of moral indignation. In doing this, I shall feel myself discharging the duty of a true patriot; for he is a lover of his country who rebukes and does not excuse its sins."

With the outbreak of the Civil War, Douglass lobbied Lincoln to free the slaves, arguing powerfully that the act would deprive the South of labor, food and supplies while bringing millions of motivated recruits to the side of the Union. When Lincoln issued the Emancipation Proclamation, Douglass recruited regiments of former slaves to fight with the North.

After the war, Douglass worked to make freedom a reality. "Though slavery was abolished, the wrongs perpetrated against my people have not ended," he said. Nor would they end in his lifetime. Many tried to pick up Douglass's mantle, but none succeeded until a young preacher, Martin Luther King Jr., then not much older than Douglass was when he escaped to freedom, took up the cause of equal rights.

"We must meet the forces of hate with the power of

love," King said, as he sought to "arouse the conscience of the nation over the plight of the Negro."

King adopted the tactics of his hero, Mahatma Ghandi, and organized sit-ins, nonviolent marches and demonstrations focusing public attention on unjust laws. As with Ghandi, King's peaceful, nonviolent defiance of local governments was met with brutality and force by local authorities, swinging the tide of public opinion toward the promise of equal rights for African-Americans.

"I have a dream," King said on the steps of the Lincoln Memorial in 1963, "that one day on the red hills of Georgia sons of former slaves and sons of former slave owners will sit down together at the table of brotherhood. I have a dream for my four little children that they will one day live in a nation where they will be judged not by the color of their skin but by the content of their character."

When the founding fathers of our republic wrote the Constitution and the Declaration of Independence, he went on to say, "they were signing a promissory note to which every American was to fall heir." That note was the promise of equal rights for all.

King, like Douglass, did not live to see the day that note would be paid and his dreams come true; but as much as any figure in the twentieth century, he made it possible. A minister and devout Christian, he refused to believe that those who declared all men equal in the sight of God could ultimately refuse to acknowledge that all citizens were equal in the eye of the law.

While others pressed on to ensure the equality King had died for, the focus of the battle for equal rights shifted in other directions. During the latter half of the last century, women, ethnic minorities, homosexual and others subjected to discrimination built on what King had accomplished and made powerful arguments for their inclusion as citizens with equal rights.

"In our land men are equal, but they are free to be different," the President's Commission on Civil Rights declared, stating the federal government's official position. "From these very differences among our people has come the great human and national strength of America."

Thanks largely to the United States, the United Nations followed suit, adopting a Declaration of Human Rights. Article One states: "All human beings are born free and equal in dignity and rights."

What had been the exception when de Tocqueville visited and observed America has now become the rule. Jefferson's promissory note has become prophetic, though he would probably be the first to note we still have a distance to travel before reaching the ideal he so eloquently stated.

In the words of Henry Ward Beecher, "The real democratic ideal is not that every man shall be on a level with every other, but that every one shall have liberty, without hindrance, to be what God made him."

Linda Martinez Alvarado, David Morris, Maggie Kuhn, Marilyn Carlson Nelson and Rob Torres are currently on the front lines of the battle for equality. They speak to that ideal on behalf of women, minorities, the aged, the handicapped and the homeless. They seek a world where all men and women have an equal right to the free development of their abilities.

Like Douglass and King, each of them would say there is more work to be done to perfect the American Dream of equality; but again, like Douglass and King, each of them has helped move our country closer to the ideal—a nation where everyone has an equal opportunity to develop their talents and be whatever they can be.

★ ★ ★ ★

Linda Martinez Alvarado

Linda Alvarado likes breaking new ground. She was the first woman to buy part of a professional baseball team, the first Hispanic to sit on boards of four Fortune 500 companies and the first Hispanic woman to become a player in the one of the most male-dominated industries in America. These accomplishments are even more remarkable when you consider Alvarado grew up in an adobe home in New Mexico without indoor plumbing or heat.

Her mother, Lily Martinez, brought water from a drainage ditch to wash clothes and took in ironing from the big houses up the hill to help pay the bills. But she always wanted something better for her six children. Ironing was work she never wanted her daughter to have to do.

"That was her gift to me," says Alvarado. "She did housework so I could study. I grew up with my parents telling me to expect bias regarding my ethnicity and gender but to not ever allow it to be the reason I didn't try to succeed. I had to do more than merely be a member of a club. I had to be a leader."

After high school, Alvarado went to Pomana College, where she applied for a student job as a day laborer to help pay expenses. For her it was a natural thing to do. She had always worked alongside her brothers, but when Linda first showed up for work, she remembers being greeted with icy looks.

"What are you doing here?" one man asked.

Female students, she was told, worked in the school cafeteria. The day laborer job was reserved for men. Ignoring her detractors, Linda stayed on the job. She found she loved outdoor work and decided it would be the cornerstone of her life.

With some difficulty, Linda found a job with a commercial development company after college. At that time, women weren't welcome in construction. She was the subject of rude jokes and the target of graffiti written on the walls of the construction site, including drawings of her in various states of undress. Nevertheless, she says, she liked being on the job. She loved watching the buildings come up out of the ground.

"When a superstructure went up, it was to me a great sense of the creative process that ended up with this structure of great permanence and beauty," Alvarado says.

While she worked these multimillion-dollar sites, she began dreaming about a small building project of her own. An entrepreneur at heart, she yearned for own business. She also had something she wanted to prove.

"I had some sense of personal mission," she recalls. "I wanted to show that women could succeed in this field."

In 1976, Linda decided to start a small construction management company. She wrote a business plan, put on her best blue suit and began visiting banks. The response was not encouraging. She was young, female and Hispanic, with no collateral and no track record in a business where women made up less than 1 percent of the skilled workers. It was a gamble the bankers did not want to take.

After six banks said "no," she got a boost from her parents, who remortgaged the family's house to lend her $2,500 in start-up funds.

"You can imagine how I felt," she says, "knowing that if I screwed up, they'd lose everything."

Alvarado Construction started with flatwork—simple paving jobs—but soon graduated to building bus-stop shelters. She did well, but quickly learned that when she submitted work proposals it was better not to sign her full name. "I signed my initials," she said. "Not only was I a woman, but I was Hispanic. With both factors I was considered too 'high risk' to be taken seriously in the construction business."

Today, the woman who could not be taken seriously manages multimillion-dollar construction projects as CEO of Alvarado Construction, now based in Denver. It is one of the fastest growing companies in the industry. Alvarado Construction's large-scale projects include convention centers, airports and aquariums. Alvarado Construction helped build the Denver Broncos stadium, the Colorado Convention Center, Denver International Airport and the $600 million renovation of the Phoenix Civic Plaza.

For her, being successful has meant challenging stereotypes while charging toward her dreams. "Because there can be so much harassment in this business, I had to hold on to a mental state," Alvarado says. "I had to strongly believe that because something had not been done before, it was no reason that it couldn't be done at all. In life you'll meet people who embrace your dreams and those who will try to stop you. You have to let discouraging things roll off and stay focused."

In the mid-1980s, while building a strip mall, Alvarado found she needed an anchor tenant. She approached Taco Bell, a relatively new franchise company at the time, and found a new business for herself. When she sold the shopping center, she kept the restaurant.

From that one restaurant came another company—Palo Alto Inc. Palo Alto Inc., which she started with her husband Robert, has built and runs more than 150 fast-food franchise restaurants, including Taco Bell, Pizza Hut, and Kentucky Fried Chicken.

"Unless you try, you never know how much you can achieve," Linda says, explaining her drive.

As an example, she points to the Colorado Rockies. She had never considered owning a professional sports team before she heard that the Colorado Rockies major league baseball franchise was for sale; but the more she thought about it, the more excited she grew about the prospect. No woman had ever participated in a bid for a Major League baseball franchise.

"It was a huge risk for a woman, especially a Hispanic woman, to own a sports team," she says. But the gamble paid off. Alvarado broke barriers again by becoming, at thirty-nine, part owner of the Colorado Rockies.

"What Hispanics have lacked in the past is not talent or ability; it's opportunity," Alvarado says. "So we must create it. The American Dream is not male or female. It is genderless, as well as raceless. It is a changing vision and a changing dream. It is looking forward. Who would have dreamed I'd be a contractor? Who would have dreamed I'd be in baseball? We have opportunities to break through barriers, but what I still hope for and long for is the day when people will truly be judged not based on where they come from, and their gender, but on their ability."

★ ★ ★ ★

David Morris

The reason his company is so successful, David Morris says, is simple: "I hire the people no one else wants to hire." Morris is the CEO of Habitat International, Inc., which manufactures and supplies indoor and outdoor carpets, mats, artificial putting greens, and floor coverings for Home Depot, Lowe's and other retail corporations. Twenty years ago, a caseworker for the disabled asked if he would consider hiring some mentally challenged employees. With some reservations, he agreed to give them a chance.

"I was a businessman and very nervous of hiring people with mental and physical disabilities," he says. "I had my fears of workman's comp and what other employees and the community would think. I was almost forced to hire the first group of people, and my employees were as scared as I was. But about a week and a half later, they all came to me and said, 'Why can't we hire more people who smile, care and want to be here?' That's where this whole thing started. From that day on, we never looked back."

Today, upwards of ninety percent of Habitat's workers are disabled. Their conditions range from autism to Down's syndrome, cerebral palsy, alcoholism and manic depression, but they share a desire to be productive and independent.

"Once they develop self-esteem and pride and forget the word 'no,' they are the best workers in the world," Morris says. "That goes from bipolar to schizophrenics and every other group."

The company has virtually no absenteeism and very little turnover. "A lot of so-called normal people want you to pay them, but if it's sunny they would rather be at the lake," Morris explains. "My people are so dedicated we have to force them to go home when they are sick. They want to be here."

The company refuses state and federal support because Morris believes this changes the nature of the relationship from one of equity to charity. He also refuses to be caught up in the government's bureaucracy and red tape.

"I hire from the special education classes that come here to learn how to work. We train them for three to four years, teach them every job in the place and then hire them. What could be better than that?"

Habitat's logo is "A Company of Positive Distraction," drawn from a comment one of the company's employees made to a reporter from *Southern Living*. The employee, a schizophrenic, was asked how he felt about working with people with disabilities.

"I don't see anyone with disabilities," he said. "I see everyone with a distraction. If you don't have a distraction, think about how much more you could accomplish. My distraction is that I hear voices, and this person's may be this or that, but we all come here and work it through together."

Proving you can do well by doing good, Habitat has doubled in size since 2001, despite a slow economy. Over the last three years, the company profits have tripled. To accommodate its growth, last fall Habitat relocated its headquarters from Roswell, Georgia, to Chattanooga, Tennessee, moving from a plant that was formerly a 50,000-square-foot chicken coop to a modern facility three times that size. As you might expect, all of Morris' special employees made the transition with him.

"In our society you're taught that a business is a cold, sterile environment. Everyone's a number and has a fixed place in the company's hierarchy," Morris says. "We have changed the paradigm. All personnel, even managers, are cross-trained. The employees see that and just want to pitch in and be part of the team. Everybody here can do basically every job in the plant, whether it's gluing putting greens, cutting rugs or loading trucks. They move around and do what needs to be done."

The secret, Morris says, is to get rid of the "us vs. them" mentality and embrace the fact that everyone has problems. "Once you realize that we really are all human beings, all interconnected, you start to understand that you are no different from the person next to you."

★ ★ ★ ★

Maggie Kuhn

In 1970, when she reached the age of sixty-five, Maggie Kuhn was abruptly retired. She was given a sewing machine as a farewell gift. Maggie never unpacked the machine, choosing instead to bring a group of her friends together to fight age discrimination.

"I had never given retirement much thought," she explained. "I felt energetic enough to go on for many years. The idea of retiring struck me as ludicrous and depressing."

Maggie had worked all her life. She was born in Buffalo, New York, in 1905 and educated at Western Reserve University in Cleveland. "In those days," she wrote, "education for women was still in its adolescence. We were given two career options—nursing and teaching—and it was expected that any career would be interrupted early on by marriage."

Maggie graduated with honors and took the path less traveled. She took a job as head of the Professional Department at the Young Women's Christian Association (YWCA) in the Germantown section of Philadelphia, drawn by the organization's philosophy of empowering individuals to change society. "Social workers back then called it 'group work,'" she wrote in her biography. "The idea was that individuals could find meaning and purpose through group association." It was an idea that resonated with the core of her being and would find expression throughout her life.

During World War II, Maggie Kuhn became a program coordinator for the YMCA's USO division, witnessing and supporting the birth of women's liberation as women poured into defense industries to build the aircraft and guns necessary for the war. After the war, she accepted a job in Philadelphia at the national headquarters of the Presbyterian church in order to be near her ailing parents.

"At the YWCA," she said, "I had worked to bring better working conditions, education and enrichment to working-class women. Now, my coworkers and I were engaged in urging churchgoers to take progressive stands on important social issues like desegregation, urban housing, McCarthyism and nuclear arms. We believed that without powerful institutions like the Presbyterian church advocating reform, many problems would go unsolved."

Given this history of advocacy and activism, Maggie's response to a forced retirement probably could have been predicted. The small group of friends who met to discuss the problems of retirees quickly grew to the hundreds. In 1972, the group adopted the name the "Gray Panthers," capturing the organization's controversial and action-oriented nature.

From the beginning, the Gray Panthers demonstrated a flair for attracting attention to their causes. When the 1971 White House Conference on Aging—a presidentially sponsored event composed of politically appointed delegates from around the country—was held in Washington, the Gray Panthers protested. The absence of a significant number of minority elders seemed to them a form of double discrimination. They formed a picket line in front of the White House and attracted so much attention the make-up of the conference was quickly revised to be more inclusive.

When asked about the Gray Panthers, Kuhn described it as being in the tradition of the women's liberation movement. "Instead of sexism, we are fighting 'ageism,'" she said, "the segregation, stereotyping and stigmatizing of people based on age."

Over the next twenty years, Maggie Kuhn built a powerful political organization and became the personification of "senior power." She challenged all policies resulting from what she called "The Detroit syndrome"—the notion that people, like cars, have a point of built-in obsolescence. "We are a wasteful society," she observed. "We throw away people and warehouse them in institutions, making them into vegetables fit for nothing but the scrap pile."

Adopting the tactics of militant nonviolence she had learned from Martin Luther King Jr. and Mahatma Ghandi, she issued a call to arms to her fellow seniors, urging them to become activists and fight mandatory retirement and other forms of age discrimination.

"We can only survive when we have a goal," she said, "a passionate purpose which bears upon the public interest. We are the elders of the tribe. The elders must be concerned with the tribe's survival and not their own. If we continue tossing able people on the scrap pile at the current rate, our society is going to be really sick."

Maggie Kuhn and the organization she started in her "retirement years" helped make a number of significant changes in the welfare of the elderly, including the passage of legislation ending mandatory retirement, the establishment of a National Media Watch Task Force to monitor ageist stereotyping, and the enactment of legislation providing opportunities for seniors to work with child-serving organizations, giving them the opportunity to make a difference in a child's life.

Maggie Kuhn died three months after the Gray Panther convention celebrating the silver anniversary of the organization she founded. She left this parting advice to those who want to make a difference in the world:

"Go to the people at the top—that is my advice to anyone who wants to change the system, any system. Don't moan and groan with like-minded souls. Don't write letters or place a few phone calls and then sit back and wait. Leave safety behind. Put your body on the line. Stand before the people you fear and speak your mind—even if your voice shakes. When you least expect it, someone may actually listen to what you have to say. Well-aimed slingshots can topple giants."

★ ★ ★ ★

Marilyn Carlson Nelson

Shortly before she was to assume of the mantel of leadership for the Carlson Companies, Marilyn Carlson Nelson appeared on a program with her father, Curtis L. Carlson, the man she would succeed.

Curt Carlson is one of America's entrepreneurial icons. The Gold Bond Stamp Company he started in 1938 became the foundation for a group of service companies that now operates in 140 countries and employs 200,000 people worldwide. Among the Carlson family brands are Carlson Wagonlit Travel, Regent International Hotels, Radisson Hotels & Resorts, Park Plaza Hotels & Resorts, Country Inn & Suites, Radisson Seven Seas Cruises, T.G.I. Friday's and Pick Up Stix restaurants.

When Marilyn, the eldest of Curt's two daughters, took over the family business, she was mindful she would be inheriting an empire that had been ruled by her demanding father for six decades.

"Just the other day," she began when it was her turn to speak, "I received a heart-warming tribute from my father. It was my birthday, and he gave me what I thought was a wonderful card. On the cover it said, 'You're the answer to my prayers.' Then I opened it and saw the rest. It said, 'You're the answer to my prayers . . . but you are not what I prayed for!'"

Her self-deprecating humor speaks volumes about Marilyn's journey to the top.

While progress has been made, we do not yet live in a color-blind or gender-blind society. Sexism and racism live side-by-side with unemployment, underemployment and poverty.

They feed on one another and perpetuate a cycle of unfulfilled aspiration among women and people of color.

When Marilyn Nelson entered the world of business, 99 percent of the senior level managers of our country's top 1,500 companies were men. Ninety-seven percent were white. The glass ceiling—that subtle yet strong barrier that sealed the ladder of corporate advancement for women—was firmly in place.

When Marilyn joined Paine Webber as a securities analyst after graduating from Smith College with honors and attending the Sorbonne in Paris, she was the only woman in the office. In fact, the presence of a woman in business at that time was still rare enough she was requested to use the abbreviation "M. C. Nelson" on all correspondence to disguise her gender.

Nelson worked with Paine Webber in Minneapolis until the second of her four children was on the way. By that time the demands of her husband's career as a surgeon had shifted the greatest share of parental responsibilities to her. Like many other women of that day, she gave up her job to become a full-time mother.

But when the youngest of her four children was old enough to enter school, Marilyn returned to work, joining her father's Gold Bond Stamp Company. She served as a regional representative until she had proven herself and then became director of community relations for the Carlson Companies.

"I don't expect to have a lot of my family come into this business," Curt said before he died in explaining his philosophy of family involvement. "I tell them to this day that they are all part of the family, and when I go they will be treated equally. But treating everyone equally does not automatically mean working in the business. If you do want to work for the company, you need to get a master's degree, and you have to work four years on the outside to prove you are capable of moving up."

Marilyn proved herself and worked her way up, becoming vice chair of the company in 1991. Eight years later, at a gala event marking the sixtieth anniversary of the corporation creation, Marilyn was formerly named her father's successor.

"One of the challenges I faced when I became more active in the senior management of the company," Marilyn says candidly, "was that I felt I was more ready for the CEO's job than my father did." While she will not say it, much of his reservation had to do simply with the fact that she was a woman. Marilyn answered with unrelenting positivism. When challenged, she believes the answer is to find something bigger than you to care about and discipline yourself not to give in to negative thoughts.

"We must summon every resource to rise above negativity and to live every day as if this encounter, this exchange, this friendship, this task is our last—the one that defines us for all time," she says. "If we are lucky enough to have more time on earth, then we'll have a beautiful string of individual days that we have spent somehow on behalf of humankind. If we're only given a few, then those will speak for many.

"My father's biggest risk was as an entrepreneur. . . . But he was only accountable to himself; the numbers were completely his. He could look in the mirror and make a decision. . . . I have to be steward of the Carlson Companies to continue to earn the support of the rest of the family and our employees, who are the key stakeholders. Because I am not the founder, I must work with the family group to ensure that they receive economic and psychological value from the company that is equal to or better than what they can get from other investments."

In 2003, for the first time, women reached a level of parity in business. The Bureau of Labor Statistics indicates that 50.6 percent of the 48 million employees in management and professional occupations are now women.

While there is a distance yet to travel, women's rights have come along way. Much of that progress has been made possible by people like Marilyn who cracked the glass ceiling and showed the way.

Marilyn Carlson Nelson, the girl who couldn't get to the top, is now a regular on *Fortune* magazine's list of the "Most Powerful Women in Business." She has been selected by *Business Week* as one of the Top 25 Executives in Business and been ranked by *Travel Agent* magazine as the "Most Powerful Woman in Travel" annually since 1997. Last year, as a tribute to her leadership and success, President Bush appointed Marilyn chair of the National Women's Business Council, an independent body that provides advice and guidance to the government on issues that affect women in business.

During her tenure, Carlson Companies have experienced unprecedented growth, but her greatest satisfaction has come from building the team that makes her success possible.

"As a business, we define ourselves as a team organization," she explains. "I want a revolution in the way we interact with each other as equals. The value in a company is the team. You can lose the money, but if you don't lose the team, you can earn the money back."

★ ★ ★ ★

Rob Torres

Rob Torres is a professional entertainer. He has worked for Disney both here and in Japan, traveled with a circus, and toured Europe with a one-man show—even though he is still on the shady side of thirty.

Rob reminds me a bit of Jim Carrey. He has a lot of the same mannerisms and energy and the same wacky sense of humor. He commands attention. Whenever we go out to eat it is only a matter of time before he "owns" the place and every child in the restaurant is gathered around, drawn to him by some magic beyond description.

Rob is a very talented young man—but what makes him most remarkable is not his talent as a performer, but his talent for life. He is the only person I know who stops every day, wherever he is, to watch the sunset. Many people talk about stopping to smell the roses. Rob actually does.

He was seventeen when we met, a junior in high school. The year before he had been instrumental in developing a drug prevention program for his school. The program proved so successful that it was subsequently implemented in schools throughout New Jersey. Among other things, Rob had helped coordinate a drug-free student dance, brought speakers in to heighten students' awareness of substance abuse, formed a crisis hot line, and was credited with successfully intervening in four instances when classmates were considering suicide.

"Rob dares to be different," his high school counselor told me when I asked what he was like. I soon found out she was right.

I asked him where he wanted to go to college. He surprised me by saying he was planning to go to clown college. I didn't know whether to take him seriously or not until the next time I saw him. At that time, he had graduated from high school and was on his way to Florida to attend Ringling Brother's clown college.

The next time I saw him, he had a job with a circus. Each spring and fall thereafter, with the circus or on his way to the circus, Rob passed through Washington and we spent some time together.

One of the first things I noticed was that every time he came through he was wearing a new coat. Every time he visited, he would disappear for a while and come back without it. Though he never dwelt on it, I could tell he had found someone who needed it more than he did.

I have since learned Rob shops predominantly at thrift stores where someone will benefit from the clothes he buys. He wears them a while and then donates them back or passes them on to someone in need he meets along the way.

"I give what I can when I can," Rob says. "For me, sharing is just part of living. We are all pretty much the same. We all have the same basic core needs. We all need to be loved and appreciated. We all want to feel important to someone. It doesn't matter the race, religion or sex of a person, we all feel the same things."

Rob lives fully and completely, savoring each moment. He loves to make people happy. He chose a career as an entertainer because he likes nothing better than seeing a child smile.

When he was a boy he fell into a neighbor's swimming pool and nearly drowned. His mother found him literally at the last moment. His heart had already stopped beating. Another second or two would have pushed him beyond the hope of recovery.

When you live with a realization like that, Rob says, only a fool would not be grateful.

Five

VALOR

★ ★ ★ ★

Timid men prefer the calm of despotism to the boisterous sea of liberty.

Thomas Jefferson

In 1967, John McCain, the son and grandson of prominent Navy admirals and descendent of a Revolutionary War commander, was shot down over Vietnam. He was tortured, held in solitary confinement and imprisoned for five and a half years. Ten years later, he was elected to the House of Representatives from the state of Arizona and then to the U.S. Senate.

McCain's run for the presidency in 2000 earned him the affection of millions of American who came to appreciate his honesty and the strength of his character. But whenever people talk about his courage during the war, he has always made a point of telling them about Mike Christian. In his mind, Christian is the true hero.

"In 1971," McCain says, "the North Vietnamese moved us from conditions of isolation into large rooms with as many as thirty to forty men to a room. One of the men moved into my cell was Mike Christian. Mike came from a small town near Selma, Alabama. He didn't wear a pair of shoes until he was thirteen. At seventeen, he enlisted in the U.S. Navy. Later, he earned his commission and became a Naval flying officer. He was shot down and captured in 1967."

In the cell they shared, McCain watched Christian gather pieces of cloth from the care packages sent to the prisoners of war. Christian found a piece of white cloth and a piece of red cloth and made himself a bamboo needle. Over the period of a couple of months, he sewed an American flag inside his shirt.

"Every afternoon," McCain remembers, "before we had a bowl of soup, we would hang Mike's shirt on the wall of our cell and say the Pledge of Allegiance. I know that saying the Pledge of Allegiance may not seem the most important or meaningful part of our day now, but I can assure you that, for those men in that stark prison cell, it was indeed the most important and meaningful event of our day."

One day, the Vietnamese searched the cell and discovered Mike's shirt with the flag sewn inside. They removed it and then returned that evening, telling Christian to come out. They closed the door of the cell and beat him severely for several hours, trying to make an example of him and succeeding in a way that they could not have imagined.

When they threw Christian back in his cell, McCain recalls, his comrades tried to care for him, but everyone knew there was little they could do. He was in bad shape.

"After things quieted down, I went to lie down to go to sleep," McCain says. "As I did, I happened to look in the corner of the room. Sitting there beneath a dim light bulb, with a piece of white cloth and a piece of red cloth, another shirt, and his bamboo needle, was Mike Christian." Christian's eyes were almost swollen shut. His fingers hardly worked well enough to hold the needle. But his spirit was unbroken. He was making another flag.

In presenting the flag Christian so honored to the

Continental Congress in 1782, Charles Thompson, secretary of the Continental Congress, described it this way: "White signifies purity and innocence; red, hardiness and valor; and blue vigilance, perseverance and justice." More than a symbol of our national unity, the flag speaks to the struggle for independence, the preservation of liberty, the endurance of our union, and the sacrifices of millions of brave men and women who have found the values at the heart of America dearer than life.

From the beginning, Americans have known that there were new worlds to conquer, new truths to be discovered, new things to do and places to go. Americans have always hoped for a better world and had the courage to try to find it.

Columbus set sail into the unknown on the *Santa Maria*, a ship that was only seventy-five feet long. Along with the other two ships in the flotilla, the *Pinta* and the *Nina*, and a total of forty men, he sailed uncharted seas for more than three months before finding land.

Columbus was followed in 1540 by Coronado, who sailed from Spain with all of 250 horseman and 70 foot soldiers. Over the next two years this small band of men marched from the Gulf of California through Arizona, New Mexico and Texas, and ultimately into Kansas and Nebraska before heading south to Mexico along the Santa Fe trail.

The Pilgrims were just as intrepid. Two ships, the *Speedwell* and the *Mayflower*, set off initially from Southampton. When the *Speedwell* developed leaks, the *Mayflower* went on alone. The 149 passengers aboard had to brave a voyage that took sixty-five days. One passenger and four of the crew died. Half of the people who made it to land did not survive the first winter.

Valor is defined as "strength of mind or spirit." Valor sustains enterprise and ambition, the foundation of the free enterprise system. It seizes opportunity, creates success and is the backbone of liberty.

It takes courage to be free. When we think of valor, we often think of courage in the context of danger, acts of bravery and heroism. But true courage is more than that, more than a series of isolated acts that flash and pass. The valor that sustains democracy glows and grows with the light of countless, continuous sparks of compassion and responsibility.

In this sense, Americans have always proceeded with valor. In 1782, one of the early American settlers, J. Hector St. John de Crevesoeur, wrote home, "He is an American, who, leaving behind him all his ancient prejudices and manners, receives new ones from the new mode of life he has embraced. Here all individuals of all nations are melted into a new race of men, whose labor and posterity will one day cause great changes in the world."

In the realm of politics and economics, our pioneering tradition is equally evident. The Declaration of Independence was a bold move, separating a small group of colonies from one of the great superpowers in the history of the world. In 1775, a tenth of the population of the world lived under British rule. The population of London alone was nearly equal to that of the thirteen rebellious colonies.

In signing the Declaration, John Hancock captured the spirit of the occasion and set the tone for the society that would follow. Instead of looking at the odds and approaching this critical moment with timidity, Hancock asked to be allowed to sign first. He deliberately wrote his signature in such a way, he said, "that the King of England can read it without his glasses." Had the revolution not succeeded, he would surely have been among the first to be hanged.

The courage the fathers of our country displayed is

hard to calculate, but consider this: George Washington had a total of 11,000 men at Valley Forge. By March, a third of his men were down with typhus, smallpox or dysentery. Half of the living had neither shoes nor shirts. In the end, Washington was left with just over 3,000 men standing and able to fight for freedom.

By the time Alexis de Tocqueville arrived in the United States in 1831, the valor of Americans was abundantly evident. He was amazed to find it even in their manner of business.

"The European sailor navigates with prudence," he said. "He sets sail only when the weather is favorable; if an unforeseen accident befalls him, he puts into port; at night, he furls a portion of his canvas; and when the whitening billows intimate the vicinity of land, he checks his course and takes an observation of the sun.

"The Americans neglect these precautions and brave these dangers. He weighs anchor before the tempest is over; by night and by day he spreads his sheets to the wind, he repairs as he goes along such damage as his vessel may have sustained from the storm; and when at last he approaches the term of his voyage, he darts onward to the shore as if he had already descried a port."

Americans are the children of rebels and revolutionaries. We are descended in blood and spirit from adventurers, explorers, pioneers and emigrants. "We are the pioneers of the world," Herman Melville wrote, "the advance guard sent on through the wilderness of untried things to break a new path in the New World that is our own."

But it has never been easy. There has never been the promise of a guaranteed livelihood in a friendly landscape. Thousands — perhaps millions — have died in the pursuit of the American dream.

Consider the migration to California in the 1840s. In the first year of the gold rush, over 50,000 people made the 2,000 mile walk across the untamed continent from St. Joseph, Missouri, to California. They waited for snow to melt on the prairies and for spring to raise enough forage for the animals, took the ferry across the Missouri river, and started the trek to a land they had only heard of in legend. The journey took four to five months, for those who made it. America, a vast and dangerous country, yielded only to the resolute and the brave.

Through the years, millions of men and women have fought to maintain the liberties we enjoy. There is no clearer statement of America's determination to defend freedom than the one President Woodrow Wilson made to Congress in 1917. Certain that American neutrality could no longer be maintained in a troubled world, Wilson requested a Declaration of War saying, "The world must be made safe for democracy."

"It is a fearful thing to lead this great peaceful people into war," Wilson said. "But the right is more precious than the peace, and we shall fight for the things that we have always carried nearest our hearts — for democracy, for the rights and liberties of small nations, for universal dominion of right by such a concert of free people as shall bring peace and safety to all nations and make the world itself at last free. To such a task we can dedicate our lives and our fortunes, everything that we are and everything we have, with the pride of those who know that the day has come when America is privileged to spend her blood and her might for the principles that gave her birth and happiness and the peace which she has treasured."

Nearly 5 million Americans answered his call and served in the armed forces during World War I. Over 100,000 lost their lives. Sixteen million Americans served in the armed forces during World War II. More than 400,000 died. Fifty-four thousand Americans died in Korea and 58,000 in Vietnam. Many more have since made the ultimate sacrifice in Afghanistan, Iraq and other distant places.

"Let every nation know," President Kennedy said in what could have been a summation of American history, "whether it wishes us well or ill, that we shall pay any price, bear any burden, meet any hardship, support any friend, oppose any foe to assure the survival and success of liberty."

Repeatedly through the years, the valor of good men and women have proven this truth. Terrible as war is, those who defend liberty know there are many things worse, and they are heartened by the knowledge life is only worthwhile when it represents a struggle for a worthy cause.

While the defense of liberty is often seen in the bravery of war heroes, as the story of Butch O'Hare illustrates, moral courage is rarer and harder to define. Margaret Chase Smith, the first woman to be elected to both houses of Congress, is as good an example as you will find.

Tommie Lee Williams, Grandma Edie and Brianne Schwantes provide a different perspective on valor, expanding and redefining the word hero in the context of our daily lives. They are probably what President Nixon had in mind when he said:

"We cannot live a full life unless we have a purpose bigger than ourselves. We all cannot expect to be great philosophers, scientists, statesmen or business leaders. But we must always seek to reach up and reach out to achieve our full potential. Some of the most heroic lives are lived by those who cope with tragedy, adversity and the daily drudgery of life, and rise above it. It is a mistake to assume we can ever achieve perfection. But it is an even greater mistake to cease trying. Without risk there will be neither success nor failure. As Thomas Aquinas observed: 'If the primary aim of a captain were to preserve his ship, he would keep it in port forever.'"

De Tocqueville was right. Americans have never sought safe harbor. In the words of Carl Sandburg, "Always the path of American destiny has been into the unknown."

★ ★ ★ ★

Fast Eddie and Butch

Fast Eddie was Al Capone's lawyer. At that time, Capone virtually owned the city of Chicago. The crime syndicate he had built on booze had grown to embrace all sorts of illegal activity from theft to prostitution, extortion and murder.

Despite Capone's notoriety and the breadth of his illegal activities, Eddie succeed in keeping him out of jail for a long time. For this, he was rewarded with more than big money. He had the run of the town under Capone's protection. His estate filled a city block. He lived large and gave little thought to the atrocities he supported. After all, he was only the lawyer.

If there was anyone Eddie cared about other than himself, it was his son. Eddie saw to it that his young son had the best of everything—clothes, cars and education. Nothing was too good for his son. Price was no object. And despite his involvement with organized crime, Eddie tried to teach his son right from wrong. He wanted his son to be a better man than he was, and that desire led him to make a better man of himself. Eddie realized that all the money in the world couldn't buy the two things he wanted most for his son: a good name and a good example.

With that in mind, he made a difficult decision. He knew the only way he could give his son a good name was to rectify all the wrong he had done. The only way to do that was to go to the authorities and tell the truth about the man they called "Scarface." With some trepidation, Eddie agreed to testify against the mob even though he knew the cost would be great. But greater than any fear for his own safety was the desire to be a good example to his son.

Within a year of his testimony, Eddie's life ended in a blaze of gunfire on a lonely Chicago street. He was last seen leaving his office in a black Lincoln coupe, heading downtown toward the dog track. As he approached the intersection of Ogden and Rockwell, another car pulled up beside him. Two men with shotguns opened fire, killing Eddie instantly. He had given his son the greatest gift he had to offer at the greatest price one could pay.

Butch O'Hare was a different kind of hero. Fast Eddie's courage was private, personal and largely unknown. Butch's valor was public, dramatic and widely celebrated.

A graduate of the U.S. Naval Academy, Butch was a fighter pilot assigned to the aircraft carrier *Lexington* in the South Pacific during World War II. The *Lexington* had been given the dangerous task of penetrating enemy-held waters north of New Ireland. From there, her planes could strike Japanese shipping in the port of Rabaul.

Unfortunately, the *Lexington* was discovered. Nine Japanese bombers were reported to be speeding toward her. Six Wildcats, one of them piloted by Butch O'Hare, were dispatched to intercept them.

O'Hare and his wingman were the first to spot the Japanese formation. The other pilots were searching other areas and too far away to reach the enemy planes before they could release their bombs. As they approached and prepared to engage the enemy, Butch's wingman discovered his guns were jammed. He was forced to turn back. Butch did the only thing he could do. He took the nine bombers on by himself. The enemy was only four minutes from the Lexington and the 2,000 men on board.

Laying aside all thoughts of personal safety, Butch dove into the formation of Japanese planes at full throttle. As tracers from the nine bombers streamed around him, he took aim at the last plane in the formation and sent it into the sea. Then he moved to the other side of the formation and took out the port engine of the last plane there.

Weaving in and out of the formation, Butch attacked another bomber from below, taking out its fuel tank before peeling off to attack the next enemy plane from above. Within minutes, the Japanese formation was shattered, and the squadron was in disarray.

When his ammunition was spent, O'Hare continued his assault, diving into the enemy's planes, trying to clip off a wing or a tail and render them unfit to fly. Finally, reinforcements arrived and what was left of the Japanese squadron took off for safety while Butch and his tattered fighter limped home.

Butch O'Hare had destroyed five of the nine Japanese bombers. Lieutenant Commander John Thack, leader of the *Lexington's* Wildcat fighters, said that at one point he saw three Japanese bombers falling at one time as O'Hare pressed his attack. "O'Hare didn't give them a chance," Thack said. "He just outnumbered them."

As a result, Butch O'Hare became the first naval aviator to receive the Congressional Medal of Honor. President Roosevelt called his performance, "One of the most daring, if not the most daring, single action in the history of combat aviation."

A year later, Butch was killed in aerial combat, but his hometown refused to allow his memory to pass away with him. O'Hare Airport is named in tribute to the courage of this great man.

Two hundred thousand people turned out for the dedication ceremony honoring Butch's memory, but none could have been prouder than Fast Eddie would have been if he were alive. As you may have guessed, Butch O'Hare was Fast Eddie's son.

★ ★ ★ ★

The modern retelling of the story of David and Goliath is the story of Joe McCarthy and Margaret Chase Smith.

She was slight, dignified and frail with white hair and refined features, looking every inch the school teacher she had been. The first time I saw her I was a boy running the senator's elevator in the U.S. Capitol. I tried to direct her to the public cars until one of my colleagues pointed out she was the senior senator from the state of Maine.

Margaret Chase Smith had distinguished herself by being the only woman elected to serve in both houses of Congress. She had served in the House of Representatives for eight years before being elected to the Senate in 1948, receiving the greatest total vote majority in Maine history.

She had a solid record and was well-respected by her colleagues for her independence and commitment to public service. She took her job seriously, holding a perfect attendance record in Congress, as well as the Senate's all-time voting record with 2,941 consecutive roll call votes.

Joe McCarthy was Margaret Chase Smith's polar opposite. He was coarse and flamboyant, with a menacing countenance. There was nothing frail or refined about the junior senator from Wisconsin.

When McCarthy came to Washington in 1950, there was nothing remarkable about him. His primary claim to fame was that he had beat another Republican of some repute, Robert La Follette Jr., in the primary. La Follette underestimated McCarthy and hardly bothered to campaign, apparently thinking his reputation would carry him through. McCarthy won by less than 5,000 votes.

In contrast to Smith, McCarthy had no previous Congressional experience and little apparent legislative interest. He arrived in Washington as a great unknown and remained unknown for first three years of his service. He was a run-of-the-mill senator looking for an issue to ride.

McCarthy found his cause at a meeting with his advisors in the Colony Restaurant in Washington, D.C. The purpose of the meeting was to find an issue that would carry McCarthy to re-election. After considering and discarding a number of others, the group chose communism.

The Alger Hiss trial was then in full swing and attracting a lot of media attention in the United States. Communism had spread to China. About the same time, the Soviets tested their first atomic bomb, raising concern for the communist threat abroad.

"That's it," McCarthy is reported to have said. "The government is full of Communists. We can hammer away at them."

Less than a month later, McCarthy tested his strategy before the Republican Women's Club in Wheeling, West Virginia. "I have in my hand a list of 205 cases of individuals who appear to be either card-carrying members or certainly loyal to the Communist Party," he said.

The speech went over so well and attracted so much attention there was no turning back. McCarthy repeated his assertions on the Senate floor, suggesting the State Department was full of Communists and communist sympathizers.

Overnight McCarthy emerged from the back rows of the Senate to center stage. Within a matter of weeks, his name was known everywhere, and he became the dominant figure in American politics. As his biographer, Richard H. Rovere, noted, the key to McCarthy's success was the sensational nature of his charges. "Simply put," Rovere wrote, "his charges were wilder than any of his peers and too sensational for the press and the public to ignore."

To cover this reckless approach, McCarthy relied on senatorial courtesy and the privileges of his office. Knowing he was immune from suit for anything he might say in the course of Senate hearings or in statements he made on the Senate floor, he let it fly. There were no limits to the scope of his accusations.

Such was McCarthy's power that a simple sentence of his was enough to destroy a person's reputation. He held two presidents—Harry S. Truman and Dwight D. Eisenhower—captive in their conduct of the nation's affairs. From 1950 through late 1954, neither could act without considering how McCarthy would react. Though no one he accused of being a Communist was ever found guilty, he ruined careers, friendships and marriages. People he named were blacklisted, unable to find employment and subjected to public ridicule and suspicion. Understandably, no one dared stand up to him for fear of his reprisal.

Margaret Chase Smith was the one exception.

On June 1, 1950, she took to the Senate floor for a "declaration of conscience." She said she would speak briefly and simply about a serious national condition, "a national feeling of fear and frustration that could result in national suicide and the end of everything that we Americans hold dear."

"I think that it is high time for the United States Senate and its members to do some real soul searching and weigh our consciences as to the manner in which we are performing our duty to the people of America and the manner in which we are using or abusing our individual powers and privileges," she said.

"I think it is high time that we remembered that we have sworn to uphold and defend the Constitution. I think it is high time we remembered that the Constitution, as amended, speaks not only to freedom of speech but also to trial by jury instead of trial by accusation."

"As a United States senator," she concluded, "I am not proud of the way in which the Senate has been made a publicity platform for irresponsible sensationalism. I am not proud of the reckless abandon in which unproved charges have been hurled from this side of the aisle. . . . I do not like the way the Senate has been made a rendezvous for vilification, for selfish political gain at the sacrifice of individual reputations and national unity. I am not proud of the way we smear outsiders from the floor of the Senate and hide behind a cloak of congressional immunity."

Embarrassed and perhaps emboldened by Senator Chase's courage, other members of the government began to speak up in the months that followed and question McCarthy's credibility. The tide turned, culminating in McCarthy's censure by the Senate in 1954 for "conduct that tended to bring the Senate into dishonor and disrepute."

Stripped of his credibility and no longer taken seriously by the press, McCarthy disappeared from the public eye as quickly as he emerged. He began to drink heavily and died at the age of forty-eight.

Margaret Chase Smith served three more terms in the Senate and became the first woman to have her name placed in nomination for president of the United States at the Republican Convention in 1964. On July 6, 1989, President George H. W. Bush presented her with the Presidential Medal of Freedom, the nation's highest civilian honor, "for her commitment to truth and honesty in government and in America."

★ ★ ★ ★

Tommie Lee Williams

A successful plumber for twenty-one years, Tommie Lee Williams remembers waking up one Sunday morning to a series of explosions in his eyes. "You've seen those atomic bombs that they dropped in Nevada," he says, "that's what it was like. There'd be a little straight stream going up and then after it got so high it would mushroom out." As he later learned, his eyes had hemorrhaged and filled with blood.

Three years after he lost his sight, long after many people would have quit, Tommie Lee started We Care Community Services in Vicksburg, Mississippi. That was more than a quarter of a century ago. Since then, he has spent all his time giving away clothes, repairing homes, paying utility bills, educating kids and, as a result, is strangely thankful for his loss of sight.

"I believe if I could have been able to keep seeing I would not be helping people on as large a scale as I am," Tommie Lee says. "I feel God has wanted me to do this. Because Tommie Lee Williams don't have anything to help anybody with. Everything that comes through this office came from somewhere else."

How is it, I asked, that you are on the giving rather than the receiving end? How can you be taking care of this community when most people would say the community should be taking care of you?

Tommie Lee sat very still for a moment. Then he leaned forward and softly asked me what I meant.

I knew what I was about to say would make him mad, but I also knew I had to ask the question. "Well, you're blind," I said. "Most people would consider that a significant handicap."

His face clouded and his fist came down on the kitchen table between us. "I am not handicapped!" he thundered. "You would be surprised at what I can do. A guy called me and said 'I heard you still do a little plumbing work.' He had a stove that wasn't working right. The top burners weren't catching, and the oven wouldn't burn high. He was thinking of getting a new one."

"I said, 'Before you have them send you a new one, let me look at it.' I went down there and regulated the two top burners. I fixed the oven and regulated the air with it to let a little more gas in. I could hear what was wrong with it, because if you have too much air coming in with the gas mixture it makes a blowing noise. If it was making a calm noise, I would call a sighted person and ask them to look at the blaze. If it is burning blue, it's okay. So I saved that man from buying a new stove. I ran the gas, the water, sewage, everything from the street to my house. I can hook up heaters or a hot water tank."

Tommie Lee went on to describe a house he had recently repaired for a widow, tearing out portions of the back and sides where the siding was bad. Then he installed insulation and cut replacement siding to fit. He used a piece of string to measure the hole and a carpenter's ruler notched with a hacksaw to cut the lumber. The rest, he claims, was easy.

Talking to Tommie Lee Williams you get the feeling that very little in life has been that easy for him. He was born in Vicksburg and raised on a farm by poor black sharecroppers. He has worked all of his life. But there is no element of complaint or self-pity in his voice. Rather, you see the steel of those who have been tested and the pride of the self-reliant.

"When people come into my office and say 'I can't do this,' or 'I can't do that,' putting up all kinds of excuses, I don't accept that," he says firmly. "I've learned that you can do whatever you want to do and be whatever you want to be. I don't do what I do because I can. I do it because I want to."

★ ★ ★ ★

Edie Lewis

There was no reason for Edie Lewis to believe Koe would be anything but trouble. Koe was the leader of the Bloods in Houston, a six-foot, seven-inch mountain of man with a reputation for violence.

Branded a threat to the community and feared even by the members of the gang he led, it was widely believed it would only be a matter of time before Koe was locked up or dead, a victim of violence or drugs or both. Then he met the woman the kids called Grandma Edie.

Grandma Edie saw something of value buried beneath Koe's tough exterior. She saw a boy who had been abandoned by his own family, told he was worthless, discounted by society and never really given a chance. She saw the man he could be.

Grandma Edie took him in when no one else would have him. The authorities laughed, saying it was only a matter of time before he would find a permanent home—in the penitentiary or underground. They told her they were afraid she might become the next victim of his violence or be caught up in the cross fire of a gang war over turf and drugs. They said it wasn't worth risking her life for his.

While there was abundant reason to fear, faith transcends reason. For nearly a year, she held on when reason said it was time to let go. She battled his past, pulling him back in, off the streets. She flushed pounds of drugs down the toilet, sobered him up when he was drunk and held him when he was sick. For nearly a year, she told him he had a future. Finally, Koe began to believe her.

When I met Koe three years later, he was calling Grandma Edie "Momma" and crediting her with giving him a new birth. Not long after that, the man who even the toughest hoodlums feared entered a theological seminary in Texas with the intent of becoming a teacher or a priest. Now he is so gentle and so soft-spoken it is hard to believe he once had blood on his hands. Even more remarkable is the fact that he is only one of hundreds of troubled young people Grandma Edie helped turn around.

"I didn't start out doing this on purpose," Lewis said. "It just evolved after I found a kid sleeping in my backyard."

Grandma Edie was living in Alaska at the time. She heard a dog barking at about two in the morning. When she went out to investigate, she found a teenage boy sleeping against her house, trying to keep warm.

"He was only seventeen, but big, like a football player," she recalls. When she asked him where he lived and why he wasn't sleeping at home, she was surprised to hear him say, "My family doesn't want me."

"I was so naive to bad parents then," Grandma Edie says. "I thought every parent loved their kid. I just knew they were worried sick with the thought he might be laying dead or hurt somewhere."

When she called his parents to let them know he was safe, she was even more surprised. His father responded, "You found him, you keep him," and slammed the phone down. The next day she called again and the boy's father was even more irate. "I told you we don't want him!" he said. "You can have him."

In talking with the boy, Edie found out that his parents had made him quit school at fifteen to go to work to support their drinking and drug habits. They beat him and verbally abused him until he ran away. Edie took him in, and over the next few months the word got around. One kid after another began knocking on her door. "I kept saying what's one more?" she recalls. "First thing you know, I had a full-fledged shelter going."

When she moved to Texas, her work followed her. The

common denominator among the children, she said, is that none of them had a decent role model or lived in a good home.

"The child abuse stories are almost unbelievable," she says. "With the child abuse and parents that don't care, parents on drugs and messing around with different partners, daughters getting raped by their mother's boyfriends and father's pimping for their sons, it becomes unbearable. It is no wonder they leave home.

"They wind up in the seedy parts of town where all the pimps and whores are selling themselves, or they get hooked on drugs at an early age. They've had a lot of bad teachers, and they don't know what else to do."

The kids she cares for are young adults—late teens and early twenties—hardened by the streets, hooked on drugs. Many of them have been drawn into cults or gangs like the Bloods and the Crips. They are the kids most of us have given up on and take pains to avoid whenever possible.

"The general public feels that once they've reached this age—18, 22, 23, 24—they'll never get it together, and it's a waste of time and money to try to reach them," Edie says. "But they don't know the circumstances that brought them to this point. If any one of them had been brought up in a halfway decent home, they probably wouldn't have turned out the way they did. It's not their fault, but they are the ones who get punished for it. It's the parents who should be punished, but they are free to go on out and do their thing. They simply don't care. It's rare that a parent will even call up to see how they are doing.

"When they arrive here I'm usually looking at a sad sight," she says. "They're hungry, they're dirty, they're broke, many of them are hooked on drugs, and they're all scared. They've never had an adult in their life they can trust. A lot of them hear about me for quite awhile before they knock on my door. When they come, it's because they're desperate and don't know what else to do."

Like Koe, all of Grandma Edie's kids are encouraged to stay as long as they need to—six months, a year, two years. While they may move on, they never really leave.

"I'm always their grandma," she said with pride. "I'm their only family. This is home. It's not an institution. The windows aren't barred, and the doors aren't locked. In any other place, the first time the kids cause trouble, they kick them out. The first time they backslide, they are gone. I just pick them up, dust them off, give them a hug and another chance.

"It's hard to stay off that stuff. Unless you've been on it, you don't know. You are going to backslide, but eventually they make it if they want to. You just can't give up on them."

That's the secret, she concludes. "You don't quit, and you let them know you care. They know I don't get paid. I don't take any money from them, and I won't take any money from the government. After a few months they realize the only reason I do this is because I really do care. Then they start caring back, and I've got them."

★ ★ ★ ★

Brianne Schwantes

Brianne Schwantes was born with thirteen broken bones. All the major bones in her arms and legs were broken, along with a number of her ribs.

The doctors told Brianne's parents she would only live a few hours. The hospital priest was called in to give her the last rights, and her parents cried. But Brianne wouldn't give up. Somehow, she made it through the night.

The next day she was diagnosed with a rare bone disease called osteogenesis imperfecta. The doctors said they didn't know how long she would live, but they were certain her bones were so brittle they would never bear weight. The doctors told Brianne's parents she could never have a normal life and live independently. They said that the best thing to do was to put her in an institution and forget about her.

Instead, her parents decided that if Brianne wouldn't give up then they wouldn't give up either. They took her home on a feather pillow, popsicle sticks taped to her limbs as makeshift splints, and went looking for alternatives.

They found a group of physicians who were just starting research on children with this disease and enrolled her in their program. Brianne was so fragile she could break a bone by sneezing, but they encouraged her to learn to walk and challenged her to grow.

Since then, Brianne has had facial surgery, leg surgery, and back surgery. She spent her sixteenth birthday in the emergency room with a neck brace, and has had, in her words, more broken bones than Evil Knievel. But each time, she wouldn't quit. And each time, her fragile body has gotten stronger.

"It's hard to stop listening when people tell you to quit," she says. "It's hard to ignore the world when it seems no one thinks you can succeed; but it gets easier. The first time you believe in yourself enough to accomplish the impossible, an inner strength is created that lasts a lifetime."

Brianne surpassed all expectations for her future on the second day of her life. In the years since, she has singlehandedly rewritten the protocols for treatment of her disease. She has established a network of patients with osteogenesis imperfecta, testified before Congress and emerged as spokesperson for this cause.

"Because of my condition," Brianne says, "it would have been easy to live a very careful life, not to take chances and not to let myself get hurt. However, that would have meant purposely excluding myself from so many of the experiences that make up human existence. So from a very early age, I realized I had a choice to make. Either I could choose to be scared and live a life on the sidelines, where I could try to protect myself from getting hurt and shield myself from danger, or I could choose to live life to the fullest no matter the consequences."

In 2003, Brianne Schwantes graduated from America University in Washington, D.C. She found a job with Give Kids the World Village, a resort for children with life-threatening illness in Orlando, Florida. Brianne comes to work each day with a certain sense of irony and a great deal of pride. Each day, she looks around herself at the children whose dreams have come true and remembers that she too was once a guest at Give Kids the World.

"People are not meant to live perfect lives," Brianne says. "In order to live life to its fullest it is inevitable that we are going to get hurt and we are going to encounter some problems. The key is to not even give yourself the option of getting discouraged and giving up. And when I do run into a problem, when inevitably I get hurt or am faced with another surgery, I know that no matter what, I won't let it beat me. No matter how hard, no matter how painful, no matter how towering the obstacle, I will be okay, and I will deal with it the best way I can."

Brianne still breaks bones with the frequency the rest of us get a cold but nothing can break her spirit.

Six

AMBITION

★ ★ ★ ★

In this country, every man is the architect of his own ambitions.

Horton Bain

★ ★ ★ ★

Uncle Jim was the black sheep of our family. He conned my father out of his life's savings, bilked friends and swindled strangers in a seemingly endless series of get-rich-quick schemes.

As a boy, I remember being embarrassed every time his name came up. While the family stood by him, I know they were all as ashamed of him as I was. My father took it hardest. He carried the hurt of his brother's betrayal and dishonesty for years.

It was sad and difficult to watch, but sadder still was the way my uncle died. He died alone, in a rundown boarding home miles from home. By this time, he had so isolated himself with his unrelenting selfishness that he was dead two weeks before anyone knew he was gone.

Jim always thought that if he had money he would have everything, but his unbridled ambition cost him everything that matters. He always thought someone else could be conned into paying the bill, but the bill always comes home. Our seemingly independent lives are rooted together beneath the surface and tied to a common source. By necessity, each life is bound to help every other life linked to it. We cannot shut others out without closing ourselves in.

I often wonder if Jim ever really thought about what he was doing. If so, how could he not know that wealth alone does not bring happiness? There is abundant evidence of that fact. Some of the wealthiest people in America are among the most unhappy people on the planet. At the end of his life, Napoleon, at one time the most powerful man on earth, wrote in his diary that he had only experienced five days of happiness in his entire life.

Goodness always precedes greatness. Happiness comes from serving the purpose for which we are intended, fulfilling our potential and, in so doing, finding God's will for us. In the final analysis, the measure of a man is not how many servants he has, but how many people he serves. Happiness comes from serving others, not from having others serve you.

The word "ambition" comes from the Latin word *ambire*, literally the act of soliciting votes. It has come to mean a desire to achieve a particular end. That end may be an inordinate desire for personal advancement, like that of my Uncle Jim and many of the corporate executives who have been in the news so much of late, or something more praiseworthy.

Ambition seeks opportunity and thrives on liberty. "Without ambition, one starts nothing. Without work, one finishes nothing," Ralph Waldo Emerson wrote.

It's hard to imagine America without ambition. "The first thing which strikes a traveler in the United States is the innumerable multitude of those who seek to emerge from their original condition," Alexis de Tocqueville said. "No Americans are devoid of a yearning desire to rise. . . . All are constantly seeking to acquire property, power and reputation."

Little has changed in the nearly 200 years since de Tocqueville made that observation. The desire to achieve is everywhere in America, the pursuit of happiness our primary preoccupation. No longer are men born with their boundaries predetermined. In America, a man's possibilities are limited only by his aspirations. To this day, Americans are constantly striving to better themselves and improve their situations.

While the pursuit of happiness drives much of our day-to-day lives, to be a blessing rather than a curse it must exit in the context of compassion, spirituality, responsibility and a governing structure designed to balance these interests. The neatness of this trick is one of the reasons William Gladstone, one of the most respected of British prime ministers, called the Constitution of the United States "the most wonderful work ever struck off at a given time by the brain and purpose of man."

Who were these men?

Jefferson called the founding fathers "an assembly of demigods." They may not have been that, but they are certainly the ablest group of Americans ever assembled for any purpose in the history of our Republic. They were fifty-five men, comprising the elite of government, business and the professions in their own states, at the Constitutional Congress. Their average age was forty-two at a time when the average person lived to thirty-seven. More than half of them were lawyers. Slightly more than half — twenty-nine — were college graduates.

The founders spent eight weeks examining ancient history and modern Europe looking for a model form of government to adopt. They found, Benjamin Franklin said, "only the seeds of their dissolution."

For just under seventeen weeks, these men struggled to structure a workable balance of power and leadership while protecting individual rights and liberty. After weeks of debate, James Madison seized the initiative and provided the solution that forged the Union and gave us our Constitution—now the oldest written constitution in the world.

Madison was a practical idealist. He was suspicious of other systems of government and skeptical of human nature. "If men were virtuous," he reminded the Convention, "there would be no need for governments at all."

Rather than try to tightly structure the relationship between various constituencies in the United States, Madison made the profound suggestion that chaos might succeed where control would fail. The solution, he argued, was to make the separate branches of government responsible to separate constituencies, forcing them to collide and check each other.

Madison's notion that a collision of interest is not only natural to governments but the source of their health was disturbing to many around him. He responded by saying, "Ambition must be made to counteract ambition. The interest of the man must be connected with their constitutional rights."

One hundred years later, Justice Oliver Wendell Holmes said it this way, "A constitution is made for people of fundamentally differing views." This idea, that competing ambitions create good government, is the central principle of the constitution. It is seen in the balance of power between the states and the federal government, as well as in the diffusion of power among the three branches of government.

It is also the safety valve for our economic system. The American Republic and American business are Siamese twins. They came out of the same womb at the same time and were born with the same values. They are so closely connected they cannot be separated without peril. They can only exist in the context of freedom, compassion, equality and responsibility.

As Adam Smith said in describing the free enterprise system, "Every man, as long as he does not violate the laws of justice, is left perfectly free to pursue his own interest in his own way, and to bring both his industry and capital into competition with those of any other man, or order of men." Ambition is the germ from which all achievement grows. Nigel Morris's ambition was to build a world class company that could be a force for good. Claude Pepper's dream was to grow up to be a United States Senator. John Glenn dreamed of flying jets and journeying into space, while Dick Bloch dreams of defeating cancer. Katie Eller's ambition is at once more modest and more grand. She simply wants to make the world a better place.

All of their dreams have come true. They abundantly illustrate one of America's guiding truths: In this country, nothing is impossible.

★ ★ ★ ★

Nigel Morris

In 1994, Nigel Morris cofounded Capital One Financial Services with his colleague and longtime friend Richard Fairbank. Fairbank and Morris felt traditional banking and financial service lacked customer focus and treated all clients the same regardless of their needs. They believed technology could be employed to customize services in a way that was more responsive to clients' concerns and financial situation.

Fairbank and Morris pitched the solution they devised, the Information-Based Strategy, to twenty national retail banks. Finally, Virginia-based Signet Bank gave them a chance and invited them to launch its Bank Card Division. Over the next few years, Nigel and Rich ran thousands of tests, eventually introducing the first balance transfer card designed to give preferential rates to people with good credit.

When the system was perfected, Signet spun off its credit card division, creating Capital One as a publicly held corporation. Since then Capital One's customer base has grown by more than 35 percent a year. Company sales have grown at a compounded annual rate of more than 40 percent. Earnings growth rate and return on equity have exceeded 20 percent each year.

It is one of the most impressive success stories in business, but equally impressive is the corporate culture Capital One has created, a culture which provides the foundation for its success. "We realize that our associates are concerned about the communities in which they live," Morris says, "and these concerns do not change or disappear when they show up for work."

Accordingly, Capital One has structured a broad range of opportunities for its associates to make a difference in their communities. An astonishing 65 percent of Capital One's associates have responded, contributing over 100,000 hours of community service each year.

"Empowering our employees doesn't take place only at the business level—just as importantly, it takes place at the community level," Morris says. "Our communities provide us with associates who are key to our achievements, customers who are the bedrock of our business, resources that allow our business to thrive and support that enables us to operate."

The best example of the power of Capital One's culture was provided on September 11, 2001. Like most of America, people at Capital One desperately wanted to do something to help relieve the agony of those directly impacted. Associates lined up to donate blood and contributed money, but that wasn't enough. Somehow, as if in answer to a prayer, an opportunity to make a difference—a huge difference—arose.

A couple of Hollywood producers put together a tribute to the victims of September 11. Bono of U2 and Bruce Springsteen had enlisted in the effort. George Clooney soon signed on, as did Stevie Wonder, Tom Cruise, Chris Rock, Willie Nelson, Julia Roberts, Celine Dion and a host of others.

NBC agreed to broadcast the event nationwide and then ABC, CBS and FOX rallied to the cause. Before long, every major broadcast network, cable network and radio network had joined the endeavor. What had started with a handful of Hollywood producers had snowballed into "America—A Tribute to Heroes," an unprecedented, two-hour live television and radio broadcast featuring the biggest names in the entertainment and music industry.

But four days before the event, the fund-raising element of the telethon suffered a major blow. The company that had agreed to support the call center backed out. The telethon operators scrambled desperately to find someone who could handle the massive task of manning the call center, but no one was willing to try.

Except Capital One.

"Even we weren't sure it could be done," Nigel says, "but our people jumped at the opportunity to help."

Four hours after Capital One committed to the Telethon on a Tuesday morning, fifty associates came together to begin working on the project. By Friday, Capital One's project team had grown to 500. Working around the clock for the three and a half days leading up to the telethon, the team cobbled together a virtual 20,000-seat call center capable of handling an unprecedented number of donations. Over 35,000 volunteers, including more than a third of Capital One's employees, were enlisted to work out of seventy-seven physical call centers.

Capital One began receiving calls a half hour before the live broadcast began—9:00 P.M. Eastern time. By the time the telethon ended on the West Coast five hours later, the call centers had received 1.5 million calls and collected $150 million dollars for the September 11 relief fund.

"We took calls from children who emptied their piggybanks, elderly people who were embarrassed that they could only scrape together a few dollars and people from around the world," Nigel recalls. "One woman called from war-torn Belfast, spending over an hour trying to get through."

It was an emotional night. Nigel, Rich, Capital One associates and most of the callers were crying. But it was also an inspiring night that reinforced Capital One's unprecedented commitment to the community and the strength of its corporate culture.

"In the future, business historians may look back at Capital One and comment positively on our earnings, or on our charge off, or on our account growth," Morris says. "But in our hearts, those of us who were here during this time will remember this night and our role in this fundraising effort. Faced with what appeared to be an impossible task during a most difficult period in our history, the associates of Capital One pulled together and poured all of their skills, abilities and hearts into making this telethon a reality.

"It was a defining moment for our company," Morris concludes. "To borrow from Winston Churchill: 'It was our finest hour.'"

★ ★ ★ ★

Claude Pepper

Claude Pepper knew what he wanted to be from an early age. When he was ten years old he carved "Claude Pepper will be a U.S. senator" on the back of his bedroom door.

After law school, Pepper was elected to the Florida State Legislature. There, in the halls of the state capitol, he met a dark-haired woman. For him, it was love at first sight.

She was a beauty queen. He would never be called handsome. He never forgot overhearing a girl tell a college fraternity brother trying to fix him up, "I will go out with any one of your friends except Claude Pepper. He has got to be the homeliest person alive." Pepper was short and fat with a face like a potato.

Still, when Claude saw Mildred, he was undeterred. He walked up to her and introduced himself, saying, "Madame, I am Claude Pepper. Some day I am going to be a United States senator, and I am going to marry you."

Mildred looked the freshman state legislator over carefully and figured there was about as much chance of one as the other. "Oh," she responded with a laugh, "Well, when you are a U.S. senator, I will marry you."

Claude and Mildred were married the day he was sworn in, one of the youngest senators in the history of the United States. Pepper served three terms in the Senate and became a stalwart of the New Deal. He was best known for sponsoring the lend-lease legislation that saved Britain and helped turn the tide of the war.

Then, in 1958, Pepper was defeated in one of the ugliest campaigns on record. He was accused of being a thespian in college and said to have practiced nepotism with his niece and sister. Comical accusations to those who know that one reflects a fondness for theater and the other refers to hiring a relative, but to the unlettered of that time the charges seemed sinister and suggestive of sexual lapses. Less comical were the accusations that he was soft on communism and the attempts to link him with people Senator McCarthy and others had branded as card-carrying members of the Communist Party.

Though he lost that election, Pepper had the last laugh. At the age of sixty-five, he decided to run for Congress. At a time in his life when most people thought he was through, Pepper had just begun. He served in the House of Representatives until he died at the age of eighty-eight.

In the Senate, Pepper had established his reputation in foreign affairs. In the House of Representatives, he became known for his domestic initiatives. He became the champion of the poor, the elderly and the handicapped.

President George H. W. Bush made a special trip to Walter Reed Medical Center to visit Pepper in his last days and present him with the Medal of Freedom, the nation's highest civilian award. After he died, Congress honored him by passing a special resolution permitting his body to lie in state in the Capital Rotunda with fully military honors. He is one of only twenty-six Americans to have ever been accorded this privilege.

Pepper's tombstone is engraved with the words he chose to summarize his life, the fulfillment of his life-long ambition. "Here lies Claude Dennison Pepper," it reads. "He loved God and the people and tried to serve them both."

★ ★ ★ ★

John Glenn was both the first American to orbit the earth and the oldest person to go into space. In the thirty-six years between his space flights, he found time to be a businessman, author and United States senator. But more than anything else, he always wanted to fly.

As much as anyone, John Glenn has come to symbolize the all-American boy. The son of a small-town plumber, Glenn was born and raised in rural America. He met the woman he would marry, his childhood sweetheart, in their playpen. Sixty years and two children later, they are still together and still in love.

Glenn's love of aviation and speed was seeded as a boy when he attended the air races in Cleveland with his father. He graduated from New Concord High School (since renamed in his honor) and enrolled in Muskingum College, but flying was never far from his mind.

In 1941, at the age of twenty, he earned his pilot's license. A year later, he left college and joined the U.S. Navy. After earning his airman's wings, he transferred to the U.S. Marine Corps.

Glen flew fifty-nine fighter-bomber missions during World War II, mostly in the Marshall Islands. He won the Air Medal with eighteen clusters and gained recognition as a leader and trainer of pilots.

After serving as a flight instructor for six years, he volunteered for the Korean War as a combat pilot. Glenn flew sixty-three missions with baseball star Ted Williams as his wing man, creating a reputation for fearlessness with his low bombing and strafing runs. In the last nine days of fighting in Korea, John shot down three MIGs in combat along the Yalu River. He was awarded the Navy Unit Commendation Medal for his service in Korea, the Asiatic-Pacific Campaign Medal, the American Campaign Medal, the China Service Medal, the Korean Service Medal, the United Nations Service Medal and the National Defense Service Medal.

Even better, because of his distinguished combat record, Glenn won an assignment as a Marine test pilot. In 1957, he planned and piloted Operation Bullet, a transcontinental flight from Los Angeles to New York that established a new speed record. He made the trip in three hours and twenty-three minutes, becoming the first pilot to average supersonic speed on a transcontinental flight.

When President Eisenhower initiated America's space program in response to the launch of *Sputnik* by the Soviet Union that same year, Glenn was quick to volunteer. Strange as it seems in light of subsequent events, Glenn's greatest handicap was his age. He was thirty-seven at the time. But he excelled at all the physical and mental tests and was noted for his stable personality and judgment under pressure. In April 1959, Glenn was selected as one of seven Mercury astronauts from an original pool of 540 candidates.

In August 1961, the Soviet Union put a second cosmonaut in space. On February 20, 1962, NASA responded by launching Glenn into space in the Mercury-Atlas 6 *Friendship Seven* spacecraft—but not before eleven false starts. Eleven times Glenn climbed into the capsule, started the countdown, then shut down while problems were investigated and corrected. After launch, there were concerns about the guidance system and the protective heat shield. With characteristic coolness, Glenn stuck to his mission, successfully orbiting the earth three times in a capsule with fifty cubic feet of space—about as much room as the trunk of a large car. The flight took nearly five hours at speeds of approximately 17,500 mph.

A few days later, four million spectators lined the streets of New York City to give John Glenn a hero's welcome. Glenn became such an important symbol of the success of the space program, President Kennedy ordered NASA not to employ him on another dangerous mission. He was too valuable to risk.

Instead, President Kennedy and his brother, Bobby, encouraged Glenn to think about a career in politics. Glenn entered the business world for a while before following the Kennedy advice and seeking a seat in the United States Senate. He was elected four times, becoming the first four-term senator from Ohio in history.

While he served in the Senate with distinction and earned a reputation as hard-working, knowledgeable and pragmatic, John Glenn's ambition was still to fly. In 1997, he announced he would not seek re-election. Instead, he applied for one last space mission.

When Glenn went into orbit on *Friendship Seven* in 1961, no one knew how the body would adapt to extraplanetary conditions. He tested the effects of weightlessness and the impact of space flight on bodily functions for the first time. Now, he argued, there was an opportunity to structure a baseline comparing the impact of space on the aging body.

NASA ultimately agreed. On October 29, 1998, John Glenn, then seventy-seven, became the oldest person ever to be launched into space.

★ ★ ★ ★

Richard Bloch

All of his life, Richard Bloch's ambition focused on the world of business. A born entrepreneur, his first enterprise started at the age of nine when he found a printing press in his uncle's attic. By his twelfth birthday, he owned three automatic presses and was doing the printing for all the high schools in Kansas City. He was making so much money by the time he left high school that he didn't want to quit to go to college.

But at his father's insistence, he sold the printing business and went on to attend the Wharton School of Finance. Before long, he had started another business—buying and selling remodeled cars. Then, in 1955, after a short stint with a brokerage house, Dick joined with his brother, Henry, in creating the company that came to be known as H&R Block.

On March 29, 1978, he found a greater purpose. On that date, Dick Bloch was told he had cancer and there was nothing that could be done about it.

"I was young and vibrant—at the top of the world," Dick remembers. "I had gone to see my physician because I had a sore arm. My worst complaint was that I couldn't hold a tennis racket. The next thing I knew, I was dying.

"I was stunned. I asked, 'Is there anywhere else I can go?' And he said, 'I will send you anywhere else you want to go, but I guarantee you we know everything there is to know about this. There is nothing we can do.'"

Without meaning to, Bloch's physician had placed a burden on his patient greater than the cancer he carried. The man who would be a healer took away his hope. "Nothing I have ever gone through was as bad," Dick says. "A human being cannot live without hope."

After five days of agony, Bloch decided he wasn't ready to quit. Now his strongest desire was to find a way to live. With his wife's support, he sought another opinion and found a doctor who confirmed the diagnosis but promised a cure. "You are a very sick boy," the doctor said. "But we are going to cure you so you can work for cancer."

The doctor was as good as his word. Two years later, Richard Bloch went home cured—and with a new ambition.

"I owed a huge debt," Dick says, "and I wondered what I could do. I knew money wasn't the answer. Compared with what the government gives, anything else is a token. I knew I didn't know enough about the cause of cancer or the treatment of cancer to be helpful. But I did know something about fighting cancer. This is my field of expertise, and this is where I went to work."

Dick Bloch resigned his position as chairman of H&R Block. He started a cancer hot line, established a cancer support center at the University of Missouri, and designed a computer program to improve the treatment of cancer patients by making the latest research and treatment protocols instantly available to all.

"Half of what the doctors who graduated ten years ago were told was untreatable can now be treated," Bloch says. "We identified every possible kind of treatment for every kind of cancer—over 800—and put them in a giant computer so every doctor in the country can have access to the latest information. People are dying not because treatment isn't there, but because the doctor treating the specific patient doesn't know about it, and the doctor's ego won't permit him to say there is anything he doesn't know."

Bloch's efforts were so successful that the National Cancer Institute adopted this program in 1984 under the name PDQ. The National Cancer Institute estimates PDQ, which stands for "Physicians Data Query," has saved more than 40,000 lives every year since—that's 800,000 people and counting!

"My goal is very narrow," Dick says. "I want to help the next person who gets cancer get the very best possible treatment. I know that's not the most important thing. I would find a cure for cancer if I could. But this is where we have some expertise and where we can be constructive."

Bloch provides all the resources for his crusade personally, with the exception of office space provided by H&R Block. He is in the office every morning between 4:30 and 5:00 A.M., much earlier than he ever came in when he was in business.

"That's because the rewards are far greater," he says. "Saving just one life makes it all worthwhile."

★ ★ ★ ★

Katie Eller

In the summer of 1994, Katie Eller opened a lemonade stand in Tulsa, Oklahoma. She had just turned ten, but she had a good head for business. Knowing there was a big convention in town, Katie set up her stand across the street, between the hall and the parking lot.

Even she was surprised when she cleared $26.27 on her first day. It was so much more than she expected, she was unsure what to do with the money. After discussing the matter with her family and considering the options, she decided to donate the money to the homeless shelter. Her father took her to the shelter the following day so she could make her contribution and see where the money was going.

"My heart nearly broke," she remembers, "when I saw a girl about my own age trying to play under a table in a crowded room."

Katie felt she had to do something about it. From that instinct, Lemon-Aid was born. Her dream was to franchise her lemonade stand as a way to raise money for the homeless. She began by first recruiting her friends and then their friends. She put up flyers, worked the press and asked for time at student assemblies. When her school was solidly behind her, she used the momentum to reach out to other schools, repeating the process and recruiting still more volunteers.

Once the manpower problem was solved, she went after the supply side. To keep cost down and maximize profits, she obtained the donation of thousands of pounds of sugar and lemonade mix. She asked local corporations to help her gather building material and paper supplies for Lemon-Aid stands and then went after corporate sponsors for the entire project.

In its first summer as a city-wide project, Lemon-Aid grew to 200 lemonade stands, raising $7,000. Seven hundred children participated in this effort. Eight years later, Katie's franchise had grown to 1,000 stands in Tulsa and the surrounding area.

In all, with matching money and corporate sponsors, Katie and her friends were able to raise more than $500,000 for the homeless shelter before she went off to college. Among other things, they were able to build a playroom for children like the one that first touched her heart and inspired her project.

Seven

LIBERTY

★ ★ ★ ★

*Liberty—the greatest of all earthly blessings—
give us that precious jewel and you may take
everything else.*

Patrick Henry

Most of us have come to America or are descendants of people who have come to America looking for liberty. Many endured great hardships to do so, leaving everything familiar behind, taking with them only the clothes on their backs, a few meager belongings, and their hopes and dreams.

For Patrick Henry, liberty was "the greatest of all earthly blessings." For H. G. Wells, it "is the very substance of life."

What is so compelling?

The word liberty comes from the Latin word for free. Webster's dictionary tell us it is: The state of being free, the power to do as one pleases, freedom from despotic control, and the power of choice.

Liberty, in other words, is freedom, and it embraces all of the forms of that virtue that we hold dear. Freedom of speech, freedom of press, freedom of religion and other personal freedoms were gauged so essential to the vitality of our democracy that they were written into our constitution and guaranteed by the Bill of Rights.

But liberty, like our other core values, cannot exist independently and unrestrained. Our core values exist in dynamic tension, feeding into, enabling and balancing each other. Without balance, for example, the pursuit of happiness degenerates into a free-for-all, a kingdom where the strong preside over the weak. Without balance, liberty becomes license.

In 1982, I led a Senate investigation of one of the largest nursing home chains in the South. The proprietors of these nursing homes were accused of neglecting their patients to the point where twenty-six people had died over the period of six months.

Our investigation indicated the cause of death was malnutrition. The owners had simply starved these people to death, minimizing food and withholding nutritional supplements to keep the cost down and maximize profits.

We brought the executives who owned the company that owned the nursing home chain before the Senate to respond to these allegations. When the hearing convened, the principals of the company foolishly tried to defend themselves by saying what they did was a common business practice. In their minds, they had a right to make a profit no matter what it cost in human terms. They tried to justify their actions by saying any prudent businessman or woman would have done the same thing.

The committee was outraged. The chairman, Senator John Heinz III, was particularly offended. Heinz was heir to the H. J. Heinz family fortune and a businessman of some note. He often pointed with pride to the fact that his grandfather, founder of the Heinz Corporation and a titan of the food industry, had helped lead the consumer protection effort by lobbying for the creation of the Food and Drug Administration even though it angered others in the industry and threatened profits.

I still remember the look in Heinz's eyes when he

turned to me and said, "I want to bury these guys. Give me everything you've got."

I gave him what I had and watched as he systematically took the witnesses apart. The hearing record was so strong that the attorney general of the state in question subsequently filed a criminal action indicting the corporation for homicide.

As the distinguished federal Judge Learned Hand observed, "Liberty is not the freedom to do as one likes. That is the denial of liberty. A society in which men recognize no check upon their freedom soon becomes a society where freedom is in the possession of only a savage few."

Liberty implies thought and choice. Choice implies responsibility. Liberty provides the opportunity to fulfill our ambitions, but it must be balanced by equality and our respect for the equal rights of others. In words that will be familiar to every first year law student, "Your right to swing your fist ends where my nose begins."

During the Civil War, President Abraham Lincoln addressed this issue as only he could:

"We all declare for liberty; but in using the same word, we do not all mean the same thing. With some, the word 'liberty' may mean for each man to do as he pleases with himself and the produce of his labor; while with others, the same word may mean for some men to do as they please with other men and the produce of other men's labor. Here are two, not only different, but incompatible things, called by the same name — liberty.

"The shepherd drives the wolf from the sheep's throat, for which the sheep thanks the shepherd as his liberator, while the wolf denounces him for the same act as the destroyer of liberty. Plainly the sheep and the wolf are not agreed upon the definition of the word 'liberty';

and precisely the same difference prevails today, among us human creatures."

True liberty consists of the opportunity for a full development of all possibilities—intellectual, material and moral—latent in man. Ultimately, it has a religious root, which is why, G. K. Chesterton said, "men find it so easy to die for and so difficult to define."

Alexis de Tocqueville said it this way:

"The American character is the result of two distinct elements, which in other places have been in frequent hostility, but which in America have been admirably incorporated and combined with one another. . . . Liberty regards religion as its companion in all its battles and its triumphs—as the cradle of its infancy, and the divine source of its claims. It considers religion as the safeguard of morality, and morality as the best security of law and the surest pledge of the duration of freedom."

Two hundred years later, President Jimmy Carter echoed that theme when he reminded us that "Ours was the first society to define itself in terms of both spirituality and human liberty."

Ronald Reagan, with his gift for cutting to the heart of the matter, put it more simply. "Freedom is the recognition that no single person, no single authority or government has a monopoly on the truth," he said, "but that every individual life is infinitely precious, that every one of us put on earth has been put here for a reason and has something to offer."

Ultimately, it is not the existence of liberty but the way in which liberty is used that determines whether liberty itself survives. Whenever we take away the liberties of those whom we hate, we are opening the way to loss of liberty for those we love. Like love, liberty is one of the things you cannot have unless you are willing to share it with others.

As Clarence S. Darrow said, "You can only protect your liberties in this world by protecting the other man's freedom. You can only be free if I am free."

Liberty is not just an idea. Liberty is power—the power to act. Therein lies much of the secret of America's success. The more liberty a nation can claim, the more powerful it becomes.

Henri Landwirth nurtured the dream of liberty from the time he was a boy in Auschwitz. After growing up in Cuba, Carlos Arboleya can testify liberty—not communism as Castro once suggested—is the most contagious force in the world. Nido Qubein came to the United States as an exchange student with $50 in his pocket, no English, no contacts and the intent of becoming a millionaire. He succeeded many times over, speaking of his life now in terms of "blessings" and "gratitudes."

Kurt Weishaupt learned the blessings of liberty thanks to an anonymous Spaniard who saved his life at peril to his own, while Jacob Green grew up hearing stories of the concentration camps and other Nazi atrocities at his grandparents' knees. Little did he know that a few short years later, at the age fourteen, he would find himself fighting the ghosts of the past in a battle for justice and the opportunity to reach his full potential.

As these people demonstrate, liberty lives in our hearts. When it dies there, no army or navy can come to its defense, no constitution or court can save it.

"Our reliance is in the love of liberty which God has planted in us," President Lincoln said. "Our defense is in the spirit which primed liberty as the heritage of all men, in all lands everywhere. Destroy this spirit and you have planted the seeds of despotism at your door."

The spirit of liberty is the key. For Judge Learned

Hand, "The spirit of liberty is the spirit which is not too sure that it is right; the spirit of liberty is the spirit which seeks to understand the minds of other men and women; the spirit of liberty is the spirit which weighs their interest alongside its own without bias; the spirit of liberty remembers that not even a sparrow falls to earth unheeded; the spirit of liberty is the spirit of Him, who, near two thousand years ago, taught mankind that lesson it has never learned, but has never quite forgotten: That there is a kingdom where the least shall be heard and considered side by side with the greatest."

★ ★ ★ ★

Henri Landwirth

Henri spent five years in the closest thing to hell that
humans can contrive—Auschwitz, the Nazi concentration
camp in Poland, and three other camps in Germany. He was
only thirteen years old when his torment began. He was
separated from his parents, his twin sister Margot and any ves-
tige of civilization. For more than a year, he was kept captive
underground at the notorious Camp Flossenburg-Komando.
Three thousand men went into Camp Flossenburg-Komando.
Less than three hundred came out.

"My father was taken by the Germans to a prison in the
ghetto," Henri remembers. "After the war, I found out he was
shot. My mother lasted almost the whole war. Two weeks
before the end of the war, they took my mother and about
2,000 other prisoners on board a boat and exploded it in the
Stuttgart harbor."

Henri, too, was marked for death several times, narrowly
escaping each time. In late 1944 as the Allies approached the
camp where Henri was kept, the Germans decided to evacuate
their prisoners. They were marched for two days and nights
away from the front line and the possibility of freedom.

Crazed by exhaustion, Henri, then only seventeen years old,
called out to his friends, "Let's make a run for the woods."
Unfortunately, he was overheard by a soldier nearby. The
soldier raised his rifle overhead like an ax and smashed
Henri's skull with the barrel of his gun. Left for dead, Henri
woke up alone in a ditch, covered with blood. He wandered in
a daze looking for safety. Before he could find the path to
freedom, the Nazi's found him, and he was recaptured.

Three days later, the Nazi's tried to kill him again. With two others marked for death, Henri was marched towards the same woods he had once sought for safety. As they left, he overheard his guards being told to "Take them out and shoot them."

"But then a miracle happened," Henri recalls. When he got to the edge of the forest he was told to stop. He waited for the sound that would end his life, but the shot never came.

"The war is almost over," he heard one of the soldiers say. "Let's just let them go." To his surprise the other guard agreed. They told him to run into the woods and not look back.

Not sure whether they meant it or not, whether it was a gift or a cruel hoax, Henri ran. He ran as though his life depended on it, fleeing for the freedom, and when he could not run any more, he walked. He ran and walked aimlessly for days, avoiding all public contact for fear of being recaptured.

One evening, in exhaustion, he found an empty house on the outskirts of a small village. He crawled inside, covered himself with straw, and went to sleep. He awoke to find an old woman standing over him. To his surprise, she said he had crossed the border and was now in Czechoslovakia. She told him the war was over.

Though he no longer feared for his life, Henri still dreamed of freedom—freedom from the past, freedom for the future. For him, that meant America.

"I wanted to get all the things I had experienced behind me," Henri said. "I wanted to start a new life. Here, you have control over your life. I had no control over my life in the concentration camps—none."

Henri made his way to the United States by working as a deck laborer on a cargo ship. He arrived with $20 in his pocket. He spoke no English. His formal education had ended in the sixth grade.

Fortunately, he had been trained as a diamond cutter. He found work in New York City, only to see his fledgling career disrupted by another surprise. He was drafted to fight in Korea. "I really thought that somebody was playing a joke on me," Henri says. "Who is this sending me a telegram from the president giving me 'greetings?' I didn't speak any English and couldn't even read the telegram. I thought someone was trying to be funny."

But looking back, this was one of the best things that could have happened to Henri Landwirth. He went into the army an emigrant with limited skills and no knowledge of the English language. He came out an American with the opportunity to go to school under the GI Bill.

Henri applied himself and learned hotel management. He got a job in a New York hotel and worked as a bellhop, a desk clerk and a night manager before moving to Florida and being offered a chance to manage a hotel in a little place called Cape Canaveral. The Starlight Motel, as it was known, was the first hotel at the Cape. It was soon to become famous as the "home away from home" for the Mercury 7 astronauts.

When the Disney Company announced it was coming to Orlando, Henri was offered a Holiday Inn franchise in the area. Guided by his unerring instincts for what the customer wants, the hotel proved to be an enormous success. He and his partners have since built three Holiday Inns in Orlando and pioneered the concept of Kids Suites, customizing the design of guest rooms to make them appealing to children. Recently, Henri and his partners have extended this concept by joining with Nickelodeon to create the first themed hotel tied to this powerful children's brand.

"I have a gift," Henri says simply. "I can see opportunity."

Increasingly, as he became successful, Henri found himself looking for other kinds of opportunities—opportunities to give back.

"I love life," Henri explains. "I shouldn't be here. By all rights, I should have died. My whole life is a miracle. I feel it is my duty to give something back."

Henri formed the Mercury Seven Foundation with the original astronauts, which provides scholarships to promising science students, and he created a family foundation named after his mother. He quietly began helping charities and those in need in the Orlando area.

Then in 1985, Henri's past and present were joined. Unexpectedly, his hotel received a call from a foundation looking for a place to house a sick little girl whose wish was to see Mickey Mouse, visit DisneyWorld, and find, if only for a few days, freedom from fear and the illness that threatened her life.

Henri was quick to agree. He wanted to help but never had the chance. The child died before the foundation could put the other pieces of the wish together.

When Henri heard the news, he swore this would never happen again. From Henri's promise has come a network of over 800 supporting corporations and a miracle called Give Kids The World Village, a resort for terminally ill children who want to visit DisneyWorld and other Orlando attractions. Over 60,000 children and their families have visited this joyful village in the eighteen years since it was created. They have come from all fifty states and fifty foreign countries.

Not content to rest there, Henri went looking for another opportunity to do some good and give something back to the country that had given so much to him. "I kept remembering when I was homeless after the war," Henri said. "I had nothing."

With these memories in mind, Henri contacted a homeless center near his home and asked if he could come visit. He said he wanted to talk with some of the homeless people there to see what he could do to help them. What they needed, he discovered, were clothes—not just the worn attire passed on by well-meaning citizens, but clean, new clothes they could wear as they looked for work and tried to get back on their feet. They also needed shaving kits, toiletries and fresh underwear.

Henri's meeting with the homeless lead to the creation of Dignity-U-Wear, which encourages stores to donate new clothing for distribution through agencies serving the needy. In less than three years, Dignity-U-Wear has generated $7.2 million worth of new clothing, which has been donated to 47,000 homeless people, half of them children. Donors include Stein-Mart, Target, Ralph Lauren and The Men's Wearhouse.

"Most people don't know what's outside the United States. We take things for granted. You have to see what's going on in different parts of the world to appreciate America," Henri says. "Here we have freedom. We have a voice. We have opportunity.

"There is no place like America. I love this country. This country made it possible for me to become someone."

★ ★ ★ ★

Carlos J. Arboleya

Carlos Arboleya went to school with Fidel Castro. "In fact, if you look closely at his picture," Carlos says, "you'll see he has a chipped tooth. I am the one who gave him that chipped tooth." They were playing football and got into an argument, Carlos explains. "So I punched him in the mouth." Even now, there is more than a trace of satisfaction in his voice when he tells the story.

Carlos was born in Havana, Cuba. When he was seven, his father, a struggling watchmaker, became ill with cancer, and Carlos was sent to the United States to live with an aunt in Brooklyn. He attended New York Public School 89 and Stuyvesant High School before his father asked him to return to Cuba to help support the family.

Carlos began working for the First National City Bank of New York in Havana, Cuba, as an office boy. He worked his way up to manager of the Trust Department of the bank and later became the chief auditor for Banco Continental Cubano. He also pursued his education, earning degrees in business administration, commercial and administrative law, accounting and commercial services from the University of Havana.

When Castro confiscated the banks of Cuba, Arboleya knew it was time to leave. He booked passage on the next flight but was not allowed to go for twenty-two days. He was finally granted permission to leave on the condition he left everything he had behind. His house and belongings were confiscated. He arrived in Miami with his wife, his two-year old son and $40 in his pocket.

Despite his sixteen years experience in banking, he could not find work of any kind in any of the banks in the Miami area. Desperate to support his family, he took a job as an inventory clerk in a Miami shoe factory, but he did not remain a clerk long. Soon, he had worked his way up to vice president. Fate intervened when he called on the bank that had the shoe company's business. The bank president was so impressed with Carlos' knowledge of the banking business he offered him a job on the spot. He resigned his position with the shoe company and started over again as a clerk with the Boulevard National Bank.

Again, Carlos rose swiftly through the ranks. Within four years, he was executive vice president and secretary to the board of directors. That led to an offer from another bank, a position as the first naturalized Cuban-American president of a U.S. bank—just seven years after he left Cuba—and then a bank of his own.

After selling his bank for a handsome profit a couple of years later, Carlos no longer needed to work. But he was only forty and not ready to retire. He joined Barnett Bank and then Nations Bank of South Florida. At the same time, he began donating significant amounts of his time to the community. He has served as an officer, director or trustee of fifty civic, community and business organizations, but his favorite activity is working with children and young adults. Among other honors, Carlos received the Silver Beaver award, scouting's highest honor, in recognition of his thirty-seven years of leadership in scouting.

"I feel I owe it to America to give back," he says. "I was down in the gutter until someone reached out and grabbed my hand. That person was Uncle Sam. I feel obligated to reach out to others."

Like Landwirth, Arboleya believes most Americans take liberty for granted. "Unless you have lost your liberty like I did," he said, "you have no idea how precious it is. When you go to other countries and you see the poverty and you see the lack of freedom and you see their living conditions, you say 'Thank God I live where I live.' Every time I get off the plane in Miami I almost feel like kissing the ground."

★ ★ ★ ★

Nido Qubein

"What are the odds," Nido Qubein likes to ask, "that a man who came to the United States as a teenager with nothing—no English, no contacts and no money—would end up a multi-millionaire, international business leader, accomplished public speaker and leading philanthropist?" He leaves the question hanging there, and you know he refers to himself.

Today Nido sits on the board of directors of a Fortune 500 financial corporation with $90 billion in assets. He is chairman of a national public relations company, the Great Harvest Bread Company, Business Life and the Miss North Carolina Miss USA program. He serves on the boards of seventeen universities and community organizations and is widely in demand as a public speaker.

The man who couldn't speak English when he arrived has authored twenty books and recorded hundreds of audio and video learning programs. He has never taken a penny from the receipts of any of them, preferring to donate all the proceeds to worthy causes.

Qubein was born in Amman, Jordan. His father had a stroke when he was five and died the following year, leaving his mother a widow with five children to support. Nido was eleven years younger than his closest sibling, so for many years he lived alone with his mother in a tiny apartment. She worked as a seamstress, dreaming of sending him to America.

"She thought I would do well here," Nido says. "America is the land that every aspiring human being who is not an American vies to come to. It's the land of opportunity; it's the land of liberty; it's where the streets are paved with gold; it's the land where if you are willing to work hard enough and smart enough, you can make something valuable of your life."

Nido came to the United States at the age of eighteen as an exchange student. While getting an education was his immediate purpose, from the beginning his long-term goal was to become a millionaire.

"That's what America is all about!" he says. "You don't come to America to check out the trees and go to McDonald's."

Qubein's first challenge was to learn the language. He began each day by writing ten English words on a three-by-five card and then memorized the spelling and meaning of those words. The next day, he repeated the process with ten new English words.

"By the end of the year, I had 3,120 words in my vocabulary," Nido explains. "The typical American has about a 5,000-word vocabulary. I was still disadvantaged, but I could get by."

While in school, Qubein worked ten hours a day to pay his living expenses and cover his tuition. He washed dishes, sorted books, worked at summer camps and wrote for a local newspaper. His career as a speaker began almost by accident when the president of his college began taking him to speak at churches that financially supported the institution.

At the end of his last year at college, the president called him aside and said, "I know you've worked hard to pay your way—but in fact, there was a chasm between what you paid and what you owed. You might want to know a doctor in a neighboring city paid the difference."

Nido said he was anxious to meet this doctor and thank him for his generosity, but the doctor preferred to remain anonymous. "That day I made a commitment to God," he said. "My commitment was that when I started earning money, any money at all, I, too, would do something to have an impact on the lives of others."

True to his promise, when he started his first business in

1973 he founded the Qubein Foundation, taking $500 from his business to give his first scholarship. Today, some thirty years later, he has given about $3.5 million in scholarships to college students across America.

"Immigrants are four times more likely than native-born Americans to become millionaires in this country," Nido says. "This is not because they are smarter or have better connections. It is because they start with the right premise: If I work hard and smart, I can make something come to be. They have the right beliefs. Your beliefs drive your behavior; your behavior drives your results. So many people here are focused on what's wrong, instead of seeing the possibilities."

Nido uses himself as a case in point. "Look at me," he says. "If I can make it in America, anyone can. People know I must know the system because I have made the journey. I came across the bridge. Not only did I come across the bridge, I built it. I didn't come to America just to check it out. I came to America because I wanted a better life, which meant, for me, wealth and well-being."

Qubein has developed a simple system to maintain balance in his life. "I invest one-third of my life in earning; you have to earn resources if you want to be able to give resources. I invest one-third of my life in learning. And I invest one-third of my life in giving and serving."

"You give not because you have to, not because someone asks you to, not because you owe it, but rather out of the heart of gratitude," he says. "God is not pleased with people who simply give back. People who view their stewardship as giving back miss the point. Significance focuses on giving, period. Not giving back. Not giving as payment. Giving is about sharing your heart.

"I use the word 'blessing' to describe what's happened in my life. I use the word 'gratitude' to describe my experience of those blessings. Those are the two words that guide my life."

★ ★ ★ ★

Kurt Weishaupt

Kurt Weishaupt saw the handwriting on the wall. The Nazi's had invaded his homeland. He knew it was only a matter of time before they came for him. With his wife, Kurt made his way to Marseilles and from there to the Pyrenees, where he crossed over into Spain. They left for Madrid with nothing but a train ticket.

The Weishaupts had converted their money to British pounds, but that currency had been declared invalid by the British because of German counterfeiting. With forged documents and without a penny to his name Kurt knew they were exposed and vulnerable.

When the conductor, accompanied by a Gestapo officer, came through the train to check tickets, he looked at the Czech passport Kurt had picked up in Marseilles and immediately recognized it as a forgery. Sixty years later, Kurt still trembles when he recalls the terror of hearing the man call out—"This is a false document!"

At that moment, a door to a first-class compartment near them opened. Before Kurt could respond, he heard someone say, "Don't molest these people. They are my friends."

The conductor stopped short, bowed and withdrew, taking the man from the Gestapo with him. Kurt watched in disbelief, not quite certain what had happened. He was even more surprised when their benefactor stood up and called them into his compartment. He was a tall man with the bearing of a patrician. He invited the Weishaupt's to join him and told them everything would be all right.

"He took us to Madrid," Kurt said. "He brought us to a

hotel, paid the bill in advance and bought us some food. The next day, he picked us up in the afternoon, showed us the city, and then took us to dinner."

The following morning the Good Samaritan returned. He escorted the Weishaupts to the train station. He told them he had arranged for their travel and purchased tickets to get them safely out of Spain. He gave them some documents in Spanish, which he said should be presented to the border patrol, and three thousand pesetas for the journey.

"When we came to the Portuguese border," Kurt remembers, "we were again asked to present our passports. Everyone else on the train had to get out. But we were allowed to continue."

Kurt never knew the name of his benefactor. Nor does he know what moved this man to risk his life for a stranger. While it would be nice to know, he says it really doesn't matter.

In the years after his escape, Kurt amassed a fortune as a stamp collector. The more he made, the more he gave back. When I met him, he was supporting one hundred different charities.

The life the Spaniard saved blossomed to save hundreds of critically ill children. The man the Spaniard clothed and fed has clothed and fed thousands in equal need. Like his benefactor, most of what he has done has been done anonymously.

★ ★ ★ ★

Jacob Green

Jacob was born with an innate love of liberty.

His grandmother was sent by the Nazis to a forced labor camp near Berlin when she was sixteen. When she got scarlet fever and could no longer work, the Nazis put her on a train to a concentration camp, Camp De Gurs, in the foot of the Pyrenees Mountains in France. Over 1,000 of the 13,000 people incarcerated there died of starvation and illness in the first five months.

His grandfather escaped the Nazis by leaving early. He came to the United States in 1938 and returned to Europe in a soldier's uniform. He was among the GIs landing at Normandy Beach, serving with the U.S. Army 5th Engineers Amphibious Special Brigade.

At first, his grandparents didn't talk much about their experiences. When Jacob was eight, they slowly began opening up.

"My grandfather heard me say I hated my math teacher," Jacob recalls. "He pulled me aside and went off on me saying he didn't ever want to hear me say that word again because hate causes war."

Slowly, his grandparents began telling their story so that their grandson would understand. Most powerful were the letters Jacob's grandfather wrote shortly after he arrived in the United States. Jacob still carries one to this day.

"Life is beautiful if we know how to live," his grandfather wrote in 1939, "if we know that our life has the purpose to accomplish things that make the world a place of glory. Life is grand if we understand that we are born to do our part to make the world a home for all. We are born to respect the rights of our neighbors, to live in universal brotherhood.

"Today we live in a world that struggles to gain and secure the precious treasures of life: liberty, justice and humanity. It is the duty of all decent peoples in the world to back up the forces who protect the rights of mankind.

"It is a privilege of the Jews of the world to join the fighting ranks of those countries which are the defenders of the greatest ideals that will ever be: freedom of religion, freedom of speech and freedom of press. We Jews are proud to be refused by the forces who want world-domination, who bring destruction to culture and civilization.

"Let us gladly accept the task that we are to bear. Let us gladly accept the challenge of the antihumane world. Let us gladly answer the call to defend the greatest ideals of civilization. We, who are privileged to live in this blessed country; we, who have seen the terror and the disaster, let us pledge our lives and all we possess to the cause for which this country and its allies fight.

"Let us pray that God will rule a world that knows not hate, but love. A world that knows no wars, but peace. A world that knows no destruction, but creation. A world where all people shall live in brotherhood, in neighborly respect, in dignity. Let us pray that the generations to come will know to appreciate our efforts to make this world safe and happy, where Jews and Christians and people of all faiths will shake hands as God's children."

Six years later, when Jacob was fourteen, he found an anti-Semitic drawing in his high school locker. It was a crude caricature of a Jew with the caption "Hitler should have finished the job."

Others had been targeted as well, but, thanks to his grandparents, Jacob was the one who was best prepared to respond. "I realized it became real if I had fear. If I was intimidated, I wouldn't be able to go to school in peace—just as my grandfather had been denied the right to go to school by the Nazis.

I wouldn't have a chance to succeed or excel. And I realized there were many more people in the same situation who were being put down, denied their freedom and kept from achieving their potential."

Jacob complained to the school administration. He took a stand and started speaking out, doing media interviews. He started a club of concerned students, dubbed Griffins with a Mission after the school's mascot, and began by surveying other students to find out about cultural prejudices and build understanding.

That activity lead to antiracism assemblies and conflict mediation training activities aimed at educating elementary and middle school students, culminating in a Week of Understanding. Under Jacob's leadership, thousands of students took part in the club's multicultural retreats, leading to the creation of an annual conference on human relations for California high school students.

Jacob left for college with confidence and a sense of accomplishment, only to be tested again in a dramatic way. In his freshman year at Berkeley, he came upon a thug in the process of assaulting two women. The women were in a subway ticket booth, pinned against the wall and trying, as best they could, to avoid their assailant.

"The women were screaming," Jacob recalls. His sense of justice left him no choice but to intervene. "I couldn't watch them being hit any more. I had to stop watching and do something."

To this day, his memory of what happened next is spotty. He knows the man turned on him. He knows he was struck repeatedly on the head with a steel pipe. He knows the police came. But he has no memory of chasing the felon down, the golf ball–size swelling over the occipital nerve at the back of his head, or the ambulance that came to take him to the emergency room. Jacob wound up with a severe head injury. The man who attacked him was out of jail on bail before Jacob was out of the hospital.

Once more, Jacob's future and his ability to pursue his dreams were threatened. He had to drop out of school and enter a rehabilitation program to relearn basic life skills. He went from being an honors student at Berkeley to hearing a counselor say the best option for him was to transfer to a vocational school. Like his grandfather but in a more personal sense, Jacob felt the forces of hate were trying to keep him from achieving his potential. Again, he refused to be intimidated.

Two years after his head injury, he entered the Coastline Brain Injury School. He had to relearn how to read and write. Then, in 2001, four years after his injury, he re-entered college at the University of California in Irvine. There he holds a 3.98 grade point average, despite the fact that he still has to have pain management for his head injury twice a week.

When he looks back on what he has been through, Jacob's reaction is not what you might expect. "I feel so lucky," he says. "I have learned anything is possible. I really feel unstoppable."

Eight

UNITY

★ ★ ★ ★

E Pluribus Unum—"From the Many One"

from The Great Seal of the United States

★ ★ ★ ★

READER/CUSTOMER CARE SURVEY

We care about your opinions. Please take a moment to fill out this Reader Survey card and mail it back to us.
As a special **"thank you"** we'll send you exciting news about interesting books and a valuable **Gift Certificate.**

Please PRINT using ALL CAPS

First Name |⌞⌟| MI. |⌞⌟| Last Name |⌞⌟|

Address |⌞⌟|

City |⌞⌟| ST |⌞⌟| Zip |⌞⌟|—|⌞⌟|

Phone # (|⌞⌟|) |⌞⌟|—|⌞⌟| Fax # (|⌞⌟|) |⌞⌟|—|⌞⌟|

Email |⌞⌟|

(1) Gender:
_____ Female _____ Male

(2) Age:
_____ 12 or under _____ 40-59
_____ 13-19 _____ 60+
_____ 20-39

(3) Marital Status
_____ Married
_____ Single
_____ Divorced/Widowed

(4) Did you receive this book as a gift?
_____ Yes _____ No

(5) How many Health Communications books have you bought or read?
_____ 1 _____ 2-4 _____ 5+

(6) How did you find out about this book?
Please fill in ONE.
1) _____ Recommendation
2) _____ Store Display
3) _____ Bestseller List
4) _____ Online
5) _____ Advertisement
6) _____ Catalog/Mailing
7) _____ Interview/Review (TV, Radio, Print)

(7) Where do you usually buy books?
Please fill in your top TWO choices.
1) _____ Bookstore
2) _____ Religious Bookstore
3) _____ Online
4) _____ Book Club/Mail Order
5) _____ Price Club (Costco, Sam's Club, etc.)
6) _____ Retail Store (Target, Wal-Mart, etc.)

(9) What subjects do you enjoy reading about most? Rank only *FIVE.* Use 1 for your favorite, 2 for *second favorite, etc.*

	1	2	3	4	5
1) Parenting/Family	○	○	○	○	○
2) Relationships	○	○	○	○	○
3) Recovery/Addictions	○	○	○	○	○
4) Health/Nutrition	○	○	○	○	○
5) Christianity	○	○	○	○	○
6) Spirituality/Inspiration	○	○	○	○	○
7) Business Self-Help	○	○	○	○	○
8) Teen Issues	○	○	○	○	○
9) Sports	○	○	○	○	○

(14) What attracts you most to a book?
(Please rank 1-4 in order of preference.)

	1	2	3	4
1) Title	○	○	○	○
2) Cover Design	○	○	○	○
3) Author	○	○	○	○
4) Content	○	○	○	○

TAPE IN MIDDLE; DO NOT STAPLE

BUSINESS REPLY MAIL
FIRST-CLASS MAIL PERMIT NO 45 DEERFIELD BEACH, FL

POSTAGE WILL BE PAID BY ADDRESSEE

HEALTH COMMUNICATIONS, INC.
3201 SW 15TH STREET
DEERFIELD BEACH FL 33442-9875

FOLD HERE

Comments:

few years ago, a three-year-old girl wandered away from her home in Iowa into the fields where she thought her parents were working. When her parents returned, they called for her and only became concerned when she did not respond.

After searching their home to no avail, the parents called their neighbors and asked for help. The neighbors scattered across the farm and searched without success for two days. Finally, the leader of the search party suggested they join hands, stretch out and march across the fields together. They did as he suggested and finally found the little girl—unfortunately, too late.

When she heard the news, the girl's mother dissolved in tears. "Why didn't we join hands before?" she cried.

The same question could be asked of our response to most of the persistent problems of the world. Is there any problem we could not solve if we all joined hands and worked together?

Everyone is needed. Everyone can contribute. Individually, we may only have a small piece of the puzzle but each of us has at least one piece, and every piece is essential. This is where community begins.

Community comes when people see hope where there is fear and decide to join hands, linking themselves with others in a common cause. Community comes when people decide not to ignore a problem or run away, but to reinforce each other and fight apathy and despair. Community comes when we realize nothing of real value can be accomplished alone.

Selfishness is at the root of all moral evils; selflessness is the goal of human existence. The path to liberty cannot be taken until we recognize the fundamental fact that serving others is our common duty and birthright. An individual has not started living until he or she can rise above the narrow confines of their personal interests to the broader concerns of humanity. A nation cannot survive separate and apart.

On July 4, 1776, our first Independence Day, one of the first acts of the Continental Congress was to pass a resolution authorizing a committee to research and devise a national motto, as well as a seal for the new nation. The task of coming up with the motto and designing the seal was given to Benjamin Franklin, Thomas Jefferson and John Adams.

Two months later, on September 9, 1776, Congress gave the new nation a name—the United States of America. The honor of naming our country belongs to Thomas Paine, who has since been called America's godfather.

During that same meeting, Franklin, Jefferson and Adams reported the recommendations of their committee. They recommended "E Pluribus Unum" for a national motto—"From the Many One." If you look on the back of $1 bill, you will note the American bald eagle is the most prominent feature on what is the front of the great seal of the United States. In its beak the eagle grasps a flowing ribbon bearing that motto.

The motto reminds us that out of many states—and many different people—one nation was born. The thirteen colonies had banded together to fight a common enemy, but they had always had a separate existence. At the birth of our nation, the concern for unity was strong enough that Benjamin Franklin felt obliged to comment on it before signing the Declaration of Independence. "We must, indeed, all hang together," Franklin said, "or most assuredly we shall all hang separately."

Many years before, John Winthrop, the visionary leader of the Puritans, recognized the challenge of unifying people with no common history, customs, traditions or previous connection. In a speech to his fellow Puritan colonists in 1630, Winthrop defined his vision of the society he hoped to establish in the new world.

"All true Christians are of one body in Christ," he said, "the ligaments of this body which knit together are love. All parts of the body being thus united . . . in a special relation as they partake of each others' strength and infirmity, joy and sorrow. . . . If one member suffers, all suffer with it; if one be in honor, all rejoice in it.

"We must be knit together in this work as one man," he warned. "We must entertain each other in brotherly affection. We must be willing to abridge ourselves of our superfluities, for the supply of other's necessities. . . . For we must consider that we shall be as a City on a Hill. The eyes of all people are upon us."

This is a large part of what makes the United States unique in the history of the world. America is the only nation composed of people drawn from another place. It is the only nation whose people are not connected by blood, race, culture or original language. Alexis de Tocqueville and every observer since has wondered how such a union could be maintained.

Fortunately, the assembly that was given the task of structuring our national unity contained some of the finest minds and arguably the noblest characters to have ever appeared in the New World. Fortunately, the assembly had George Washington as its president.

The documents they developed—the Constitution and the Bill of Rights—defined the structure of our government, our citizens' relationship to their government and our relationship to each other. As Americans, we are asked to balance our individual interests with the common good, our ambition with compassion, enterprise with responsibility, liberty with spirituality.

Despite the obvious success of their initial efforts, the founders of our nation continued to express concern for our unity. "The unity of government, which constitutes you one people," George Washington said in his farewell address, "is a main pillar in the edifice of your real independence . . . and that very liberty, which you so highly prize."

At his inauguration after, a bitter and partisan election, Jefferson said, "Let us, then, fellow citizens unite with one heart and mind." Playing the peacemaker, he reminded the contending forces that "every difference of opinion is not a difference of principle."

"If there be any among us who would wish to dissolve this Union," he said, "or to change its republican form, let them stand undisturbed as monuments of safety with which error of opinion can be tolerated where reason is left free to combat it."

Shortly after the Civil War, when the strength of the union was sorely tested, a Boston magazine called the *Youth's Companion* created and published a twenty-two word recitation for school children to use to commemorate the 400th anniversary of Columbus's discovery of America. Understandably, the issue of unity was very much on their minds. What they created was the earliest version of what we now know as the Pledge of Allegiance.

The pledge they developed has been revised several times through the years and was not adopted officially until 1942. It was revised again in 1954 when the words "under God" were added; but the focus of the pledge in every version from the first to the last has been the request to pledge allegiance to the flag of the United States of America and what it represents: *one nation, indivisible, with liberty and justice for all.*

Concerns for national unity remained well into the twentieth century. President Eisenhower's second inaugural address included the hope that "may we know unity—without conformity." President Kennedy in his inaugural address reminded us that "United, there is little we cannot do. . . . Divided, there is little we can do." President Johnson followed suit, saying, "We are one nation and one people. Our fate as a nation and our future as people rests not upon one citizen, but all citizens."

America is a ragtag nation, built from the flotsam and jetsam, the scraps and misfits of the world. At times the pieces don't seem to fit, and our individual interests, our determined pursuit of success and happiness, seems to overwhelm our sense of community. But when we are tested, as we were on September 11, 2001, at Pearl Harbor and during the Civil War, the spirit of America rises, and there can be no doubt we are one people, crying with one voice: "United we stand!"

At times like these, we are reminded that our true interest is a mutual interest. The doctrines that would divide us, the people that put race against race, religion against religion, class against class, and worker against employer are false and doomed to fail.

Father Mychal Judge demonstrated his unity with the people he served by walking into the fire on September 11. He died in a hail of debris as he knelt in prayer for his fallen comrades. With the same instinct, Lois Lee has taken up the cause of teenage prostitutes, saving 10,000 girls from the street. "I just dare anyone to mess with my girls," she says.

Lowell Bartels found himself in the disabled people he helps, while Hugh Jones, a successful banker, found meaning and purpose in his life thanks to a little girl. He thought they were separated by age, language and culture but found she was closer to him than he would have ever dreamed possible.

Jason Crowe, at the age of seventeen, probably knows more about solidarity and has done more to achieve that end than most of us can imagine.

Each of these people know we are one. Hopefully, there is a little of all of them in each of us.

★ ★ ★ ★

Mychal F. Judge, O. S. F.

Mychal Judge always dreamed of being a firefighter or priest. As chaplain of the New York City Fire Department, he had an opportunity to do both.

The child of Irish immigrants who ran a rooming house, Judge watched his father die from a long, painful illness. At the age of six, he went to work as a shoeshine boy on the streets of Manhattan to help make ends meet.

Speaking of that time and its influence on the direction of his life, he told a New Jersey paper, "When tragedies strike us at an early age, maybe religion takes on a greater meaning. The closer the tragedy is to our heart and home, the more likely faith is to form, because we have been tested and tried, and from that comes faith."

Judge entered a Franciscan seminary at the age of fourteen, beginning a religious career that spanned forty-six years and involved him in everything from efforts to bring peace to Northern Ireland to conducting masses for players at Yankee Stadium and visiting the White House during the administrations of three presidents. Proud of his calling and disinterested in material things, he wore his friars robe wherever he went.

"He had no use—none—for physical things," said Steven McDonald, a police officer paralyzed by a gunshot who accompanied Father Mike to Belfast. "Give him a cashmere sweater, and it would wind up on the back of a homeless person. But go to him with a troubled soul, and he would listen intently as long as it took."

Another good friend Michael Duffy, O.F.M., described Father Mike this way: "So many people loved Judge because he treated everyone like family. At funerals, he never just opened the book and started praying for people. He made it really personal. Countless people told me that on birthdays, anniversaries or whatever, they would get a little note from him. He was in everyone's lives. Whatever was significant, he'd write them a little note about it or give them a telephone call. Everyone considered him family."

Many people point to his response to the crash of TWA Flight 800 in the water east of Long Island as an example of his compassion. When he heard the news, Father Mike rushed to be of assistance. He kept coming back daily for two weeks, driving from Manhattan to the Ramada Inn near J.F.K. International Airport, spending twelve hours a day counseling and comforting the friends and families of the 230 people lost.

Father Mike was always there for those in need, so it was no surprise that he immediately rushed to the scene when he heard what had happened at the World Trade Center. Former Mayor Giuliani recalls seeing him arrive and grabbing his arm. "Mychal, please pray for us," the mayor said.

Father Mike looked at him with a big grin and said, "I always do."

For Judge, there were no boundaries between himself and the people. Whoever you were, wherever you were, whether you were rich and powerful or poor, sick and weak, you were one of God's children. He went where he was needed and did what he had to do. On September 11, that took him into hell and out the other side.

Father Mike was killed while administering the last rites to a badly injured firefighter and a woman trapped in the stairway of Tower 1. He was hit by falling steel and concrete after taking off his helmet to pray with his fallen comrade.

The image of tearful rescue workers removing Father Mike's body from the debris is one of the more enduring images of those tragic days. Out of their great respect and in the midst of great turmoil, the firemen took his body and carried it into a church. Instead of leaving it in the vestibule, they went up the center aisle and placed it near the alter. They covered his body with a sheet, carefully placed his stole and his fire badge on his chest, and then knelt down to pray before rushing back to continue their work.

St. Francis said, "Teach the gospel always. If necessary, use words." It is most appropriate, therefore, that Father Judge's memorial service was held at the Church of St. Francis of Assisi. Thousands of mourners came, filling every seat, spilling into the lobby, down the stairs and into the street.

It was a fitting tribute to a man who would rather be a sermon than preach one. Ironically, he probably never knew his life was his greatest message.

"God was taking 250 firefighters to heaven," one of the firefighters would later say, "and he needed someone there to help him."

★ ★ ★ ★

Hugh H. Jones

Hugh H. Jones Jr. is a banker. He has spent a lifetime in that business, first with Chemical Bank then with Barnett Bank, where he rose to the position of chairman and CEO of the bank in Jacksonville, Florida.

A year after Hugh was made chairman, the son of a friend underwent unsuccessful heart surgery and died. Looking for a way to help channel his friend's grief and draw something positive out this negative experience, Hugh began investigating the possibility of establishing a memorial heart program that would benefit other kids in need. When he learned there was no real need for such a program in the United States, his thoughts turned to Korea. A veteran of the Korean War, Hugh knew there were thousands of children in Korea who needed heart surgery.

"The first children we helped arrived on a Friday in March 1985," Hugh remembers. "Two children came in together—a seven-year-old boy and a six-year-old girl named Young Joo Yoo. I still have vivid memories of carrying the little girl off the plane, getting the children in the car and bringing them home."

Hugh did not speak Korean and had no idea how he would communicate with these kids, but he was told not to worry. Sure enough, with a combination of drawing pictures and pointing, Hugh and his wife were able to settle the children in and make them comfortable.

Sunday afternoon, Hugh took Yoo to University Hospital to prepare for surgery Monday morning. He stayed with her until she was asleep and went home late Sunday night. He tried to sleep, but could not. He found himself growing increasingly concerned about the surgery.

"I think I was more scared than she was," Hugh remembers. "At about 4:00 A.M., I simply got in my car and went to the hospital to sit by my little girl."

As the nurses came to take the girl to the operating room, Hugh saw tears in her eyes for the first time.

"That's when I think a miracle happened," Hugh says.

The girl turned around and lifted her arms up to Hugh. By the time he picked her up, there were tears in his eyes as well. When he tried to put her down on a mobile stretcher, he found he could not. Instead, he carried her to the operating room, hugging her tightly all the way.

"Those three or four minutes changed my life. There was a cultural difference between us, a language difference, a color difference and a heck of an age difference, but in those few precious moments I realized none of that mattered. All that really matters is love."

Yoo broke through all the superficial barriers that separated the two of them and refocused Hugh's life. Over the next ten years he arranged life-saving surgery for seventy Korea children. Two local hospitals agreed to perform the surgeries. USAir agreed to provide transportation. Friends on both ends agreed to help make the necessary arrangements to get the children to America, take care of them and see them home safely.

At the same time, inspired by this little girl, Hugh established an unprecedented bank-wide employee volunteer program called the Community Involvement Initiative. Under Hugh's direction, all the bank's 1,000 employees were asked to put something back into the community through volunteer programs of their own design.

Hugh's initiative led Barnett's employees to contribute more than 40,000 hours to community projects. Hugh personally took the lead in establishing a Ronald McDonald House.

He also cochaired the city's children's campaign, organized a local chapter of a wish-granting group for terminally ill children, helped build houses for Habitat for Humanity and was a pillar of the local United Way. Hugh retired from the bank a few years ago, but his community involvement continues.

"That little girl taught me the most important lesson of my life," Hugh said. "I only regret I didn't learn it earlier. Up to the time I was fifty years old, I worked hard and focused on doing well for the bank, our clients and myself. I measured progress by the investments I made and the income we received. Now what's important to me is 'psychic income'— the feeling that I get when I know I can make a difference in someone's life."

★ ★ ★ ★

The girl looked like nothing so much as what she was—an awkward adolescent, with pale hair and a plump body trying to make the painful transaction into adulthood—and nothing so little as what she had been—a prostitute working the streets of L.A.

This was no *Pretty Woman* fantasy of happily ever after for the hooker with a heart of gold. This was the cold, hard reality of a young girl forced to live on the streets because the streets were safer than her home, the kindness of strangers more constant and reliable than the concern of her own kin.

In testimony to the depth of the scars left by her childhood, the first place she worked were the quiet streets of the small town where her father served as sheriff.

"Didn't it occur to you that he was bound to find out?" I said.

"Didn't it occur to you that maybe that is why I did it?" she responded.

The girl was one of a dozen I met at Children of the Night and one of ten thousand Lois Lee, the program's founder, has rescued from the streets. In the process, my perception of prostitution was forever changed. Until that time, I always looked down or looked away.

"Basically, I just dare anyone to mess with my kids," Lois Lee says. When she says "anyone" there's firmness to her mouth and a glint in her eye that tells you she means it. Lois will take on anyone—pimps and politicians, cops and madams—to protect her kids.

Lois Lee knows more about teen prostitutes and prostitution

than anyone in the country. Her interest began with a graduate school research project at UCLA. As she got to know the girls, some of the older ones—a girl of eighteen is a veteran on the streets—said it's really too late for us, but you've got to do something about the kids.

"I'd meet these kids on the street and say, if you ever need anything, call me," Lois said. To her surprise they did. Over the next three years more than 250 kids came through her house.

"Some of them thought as soon as I finished my dissertation I would put them back on the streets like everyone else. And I said, 'No, I'll set up a program for you,'" she recalls. That program became known as Children of the Night and is located on the outskirts of Hollywood.

Before I met Lois and visited her place I had an opinion of prostitutes and prostitution probably shared by millions of Americans. My judgments were colored by questions of morality and perceptions of greed, laziness and lack of self-respect. Prostitutes were sleazy people I passed with discomfort in a tacky part of town on my way somewhere else. I half believed those who said that prostitution is a victimless crime. After all, no one was forcing anyone to do anything. It was just another economic exchange—time for money.

If you see Lois's kids, this economic analysis is hard to sustain. Her kids have been abused and victimized at every level of our society. Most of them were sexually abused as small children.

"They are raped," Lois says. "They are beaten and cut up, sodomized. They are subjected to AIDS and everything else you can imagine. There is nothing victimless about it. People just don't go out on the streets and say, gee, I think I'll be a prostitute today."

It is more than a personal transaction between two strangers. It is an immense problem that nobody wants to talk about and everyone wants to cover up. Each year, about a million and a half children run away from home. A third, by a conservative estimate, get involved in some kind of prostitution or have a brush with pornography.

The solution, Lois says, is unconditional love. "We don't punish them. We are there for them, regardless of the choices they make. If they want our help, we are here for them. And if they want to go back on the streets, we understand that they have their reasons, and they know we are still here for them.

"We don't have any magic wand. We don't do any therapy here. But if you ask any kid I've worked with at any stage of the game, they will tell you, 'I turned around because she's there for me, because she loves me, because she is my mom.' It's just the basics. It's one, two, three."

Lois's message is that love is not love if it comes with conditions, claims or controls. Subtly, she reminds us we are no different.

Much of what most of us do, we do for love. Many of us live with the illusion that we can buy love with good behavior, good grades, good jobs, pretty things, success and money. Often, we become what our parents want us to become, do what our children want us to do, with the illusion that they will love us ever more.

Like Lois's kids, we must learn that love can never be bought but is always present. Love is the gift of a willing heart, or it is nothing. There is no distance between "us" and "them."

★ ★ ★ ★

Lowell Bartels

Early on, Lowell Bartels established a reputation in his community for helping any way he can. He is the one who brings doughnuts to school at the end of test week to help kids celebrate the end of the ordeal. He is the one who holds Christmas dinner for people who have nowhere to go. He is the one who visits people in the nursing home when there is no one else there.

In 1983, Lowell purchased a thirty-four-acre farm in Helena, Montana, for a group of developmentally disabled children and adults. He remodeled the farmhouse with the intent of starting a program he now calls The Farm in the Dell.

The Farm in the Dell is designed to give residents an opportunity to make a living while they learn to live on their own. With his own rural upbringing in mind, Lowell envisioned a place where developmentally disabled people could live and work together with surrogate parents. Profits from the various agricultural enterprises would help support the ongoing operations of the farm.

Helena's Farm in the Dell opened in 1989. It now houses twenty-two residents and has provided an opportunity for more than fifty people with disabilities to perform meaningful work and gain vocational skills. There is a two-year waiting list of people wishing to live and work at the Farm.

Residents participate in a full range of experiences that are common to the lifestyle of working and maintaining a small farm in Montana. Workers plant, cultivate and harvest flowers and vegetables; tend the animals in the petting zoo and boarding kennel; assemble vases of fresh flowers for local restaurants; water and weed the five-acre pumpkin patch; dry and package flowers for floral potpourris; bake and package People Cracker treats for dogs; and manufacture fire-starters from recycled newspaper.

The centerpiece of the Farm is a greenhouse, where sophisticated technology and professional advice helps residents produce 15,000 pounds of hybrid tomatoes each season. Sold in local stores, the tomatoes attract a premium price because of their quality and place of origin.

My tour of the Farm in the Dell was lead by Jimmy, a blind eight-year-old boy who came there for day-care and training. With obvious pride, Jimmy walked us through the Farm and explained the way things operated. In the greenhouse he found a small platform on wheels that looked like an overgrown skateboard and said, "This is my job." During the summer, others would pick the ripe fruits and pass them down to the center aisle. Jimmy came down the center aisle with his cart, gathered them, and took them forward to the place where others could pack them for shipment and sale.

In the fall, Jimmy helped sell pumpkins and gave tours to school groups interested in seeing how a farm operates. In his spare time, he liked to hang out at the petting zoo and take care of the animals.

"The petting zoo actually began with the intent to produce some livestock for market," Lowell said with some chagrin. "But we quickly found out that wouldn't work. The children became too attached to the animals, so we changed directions."

Bartels eventually sold his business to focus full-time on The Farm in the Dell. The program had become so successful it expanded to three other communities in Montana. There were also programs being started in four other states.

In 1998 Montana formed a sister-state relationship with Kyrgyzstan as part of the NATO's Partnership for Peace program to help the newly independent country develop a health care system, hospitals, emergency services, and services for the disabled and mentally ill. Among other challenges, the program found that, as a matter of practice, the mentally ill of this newly independent nation were shut away in small rooms, provided limited medical attention and hidden from the rest of society. The life span in one of these institutions was said to be little more than a year.

Bartels was recruited to help Kyrgyzstan lead its mentally and physically disabled citizens toward equality. With the help of the Montana National Guard, he agreed to help build a prototype Farm in the Dell. He also agreed to help develop a training facility in Bishkek, Kyrgyzstan, to educate its people about the care of people with mental and physical handicaps. With characteristic enthusiasm, Bartels kicked off his campaign by perching on a platform the size of a compact car fifty feet above Helena's busiest street for 120 hours to raise seed money for the effort.

Today, the Kyrgyzstan chapter of Farm in the Dell is the only program in that country that employs handicapped individuals. Now, Lowell is trying to help educate the people of this fledgling nation on the potential of those with mental and physical handicaps.

"I always dreamed of spreading Farm in the Dell across the country," Bartels said, "but I never dreamed the seed we planted in Helena, Montana, would take root so far away from home."

★ ★ ★ ★

Jason Crowe

When he was nine, Jason Crowe lost his grandmother to cancer. He felt like part of him died with her.

"I couldn't concentrate on anything because my mind kept going back to Nanny," he recalls. "I was feeling helpless—like I had no control over my life. Things happened to me I didn't like, but I couldn't stop them."

Jason, who is so precocious his parents put him in the second grade at age five, felt he had to do something to take control of some part of his life. He decided he wanted to help produce a cure for cancer so no other kid would have to suffer the pain he was feeling. The best way to do that, he concluded, was to raise money for cancer research.

He thought about his grandmother's passion for reading and decided to pay tribute to her and raise money by publishing a newspaper for young people. He began by researching, writing and editing articles on conservation, nonviolence, religious tolerance, racial unity and animal rights—all with a viewpoint that children can help make the world a better place. He then peddled his newspaper door-to-door in his neighborhood.

Five years later, the paper he began by going door-to-door in his own neighborhood has readers in twenty-nine states and nineteen foreign countries. The proceeds go to the American Cancer Society.

In 1997, when Jason was ten, one of his foreign readers told him the story of Vedran Smailovic. Smailovic witnessed the massacre of twenty-two people standing in a bread line outside his apartment in Sarajevo. The following day, he retaliated by going to the site of the massacre and firing back. The weapon he chose was his cello; his ammunition, the harmony of his music.

Vedran was the principal cellist with the Sarajevo Opera Company before civil war turned the city into a war zone. Dressed in his tuxedo and bow tie, Vedran went to the crater created by the bomb that killed his neighbors and friends. He sat on a camp stool and played Tomaso Albinoni's Adagio in G Minor for twenty-two consecutive days—one for every innocent life lost. He began his recital at 4:00 P.M., the moment the bomb had dropped, and played through the night, ignoring the sniper fire and the artillery that often accompanied his solo performances.

Moved by this story, Jason felt he had to keep the music alive. He responded by organized a peace concert at a local university. A year later, he founded an organization called The Cello Cries On to involve other kids in the movement for peace. Together, they commissioned the Children's International Peace and Harmony Statue—a gift from the children of the world to the children of Bosnia.

"Because of my own heartache," he says, "I have become more attuned to the heartache of others. Because of my healing, I want to bring healing to others."

Nine

ENTERPRISE

★ ★ ★ ★

Nothing checks the spirit of enterprise in America.

Alexis De Tocqueville

Arthur Flemming was a member of the cabinet in the Eisenhower administration, where he got to know then-Vice President Richard M. Nixon. When Nixon began his first campaign for president, he asked for and received Flemming's help.

Near the end of that campaign, Flemming found himself with Nixon in California. The combination of Nixon's strong showing there and a recent statement on Nixon's behalf by Eisenhower had drawn the election unpredictably close. The polls showed Kennedy and Nixon in a dead heat.

Both Nixon and Flemming knew the campaign was for all intents and purposes over.

As he considered the possibility that he might well lose, Nixon fixed his attention on polling data showing a significant shift in his favor after Ike's endorsement.

"Maybe I should have asked Ike to get more involved in the campaign," Nixon said, "but he is the president. It didn't seem appropriate for me to make any demands on his time."

A week later, Flemming was in the Oval Office meeting with Eisenhower. The election was by then over and

Nixon had, in fact, lost one of the closest elections in history.

"It's too bad," Eisenhower said as they discussed the outcome. "I really think I could have helped him. If only he had asked."

To the end of his days, Flemming remained convinced Nixon lost simply because he couldn't face the possibility of a personal rejection. And on that one decision, the entire direction of modern history may have turned.

In our personal and professional lives, no less than in politics, risks must be taken. The person who risks nothing, does nothing, has nothing, is nothing. If all we do is to try to avoid defeat, we can never claim victory. Without extending ourselves, we simply cannot learn, feel, change, grow, love or live.

The greatest regret in life is the knowledge that we may not have done all that we could have done, the fear we have not given enough, the sense that we have never fully become ourselves. The greatest risk in life is to risk nothing.

If ambition is desire, enterprise is action. Enterprise is work, particularly any task that is difficult, complicated or risky. Enterprise is the willingness to step out into the unknown with faith and confidence.

Enterprise is a fundamental part of our nature. In the words of Arnold W. Craft, "America grew great from the seed of the will to do and dare, the will to get up and go on and not to quit after we had erred and fallen; the will to struggle to our feet and plod along and not give up and lie down when we wavered and stumbled from fatigue."

The spirit of enterprise in America is broad enough to embrace some of the largest corporations in the world, as well as many of the smallest. Half of the twenty largest corporations in the world are based in the United States. At the same time, there are over

16 million one-person businesses in this country, which collectively add upwards of $700 billion to our economy. Every year, 4 million new business are created in the United States, many of them small businesses initiated by families and individuals trying to get ahead.

The United States accounts for about a third of the total gross domestic product of the globe. Our per capita income is about $25,000 a year. Israel, the sixteenth wealthiest country in the world, has a per capita income of about $14,000. Per capita income in the United States is greater than the combined per capita income of more than a quarter of the nation states in the world.

One American, Bill Gates, has a net worth greater than half of the nations in the world. Gates, the world's rich-· est man, has amassed a fortune estimated at about $35 billion dollars. The total population of the planet at the end 2003 was just over six billion. Gates could give five dollars to every man, woman and child on the globe and still have about $40 million left. End to end in dollar bills, his fortune would take you to the moon and back seven times.

Explaining America's entrepreneurial nature, Alexis de Tocqueville said, "The whole life of an American is passed like a game of chance, a revolutionary crisis or a battle. As the same causes are continually in operation throughout the country, they ultimately impart an irresistible impulse to the national character."

De Tocqueville was right. Americans are more enterprising and work harder than anyone in the industrialized world. We work longer, take less vacation and retire later. The average American works about 2,000 hours a year—100 hours a year more than Australian, Canadian, Japanese and Mexican workers, 300 hours more than the British, 400 hours more than the French and 500 hundred hours more than the Irish.

While work hours have actually declined in the rest of the industrialized world, Americans are working harder than ever. In 1990, Americans worked an average of a month more per year than we did in 1970. We are now working an average of a week more than we did in 1990.

At the same time, the percentage of people who work in America has increased dramatically as women have entered the workforce in growing numbers. In 1952, only 30 percent of women held a job. Now they make up nearly half of the U.S. labor force. Before World War II, working women were mainly single or immigrants new to this country. Now, more than two thirds of all married women with children work. In all, more than three fourths of married employees have partners who also work.

With the development of cell phones and other technology, many Americans seem to work all the time, leaving less time for family responsibilities and personal activities. Mothers now spend less than an hour a day engaged in personal activities—half of what they did twenty years ago. Fathers spend slightly more than an hour a day on personal time—fifty-four minutes less than twenty years ago.

It is hard to explain, particularly to those abroad, why we work so hard. The stress on individuals and the strain placed on families is clearly evident. There is hardly an issue of any consumer magazine of general interest that does not contain at least one article discussion the problems of balancing work and family. Personal relationships, child care and all other aspects of family life are affected by our work ethic.

While many of us feel working so hard is not a matter of choice, outsiders are not so sure. Lawrence Johnson, an economist with the International Labour Organization, believes a lot of it has to do with the

American psyche. He says, "Americans define themselves by their work."

The key, therefore, is to do work you are proud of doing. While the object of business is to make money, that is not the object of life. Your work is your love made visible. We must not only give what we have, we must give what we do. Every career that matters, every profession that fulfills, every business that succeeds over the long-term, somehow makes things better for others. There is pride and dignity in any activity that helps. There is satisfaction, joy and fulfillment in any job worth doing.

Paul Newman, Mimi Silbert, Bob Pamplin, Wally Amos and Nick Walters are among the most enterprising people in America. They work because they want to and love what they do. Newman has created an innovative approach to business and charity he calls "shameless exploitation in pursuit of the common good." Mimi Silbert has helped turn 20,000 hardened criminals into self-supporting, tax-paying citizens.

Pamplin, who made his first million while still in college, is a true Renaissance man with five occupations and eight degrees, while Wally Amos pioneered the boutique cookie business and has since started a number of other businesses. His is the "face that launched a thousand chips." He is the man who made chocolate chip cookies "famous."

Before graduating from college, Nick Walters had raised more than $1 million for his favorite charity. He is now up to $2 million and, at the age of twenty-four, has already started three businesses.

As these people demonstrate, America does not rest. We must go forward. In the words of President Theodore Roosevelt, "We do not retreat and we are not content to stand still."

★ ★ ★ ★

Paul Newman was born in Shaker Heights, Ohio, on January 26, 1925, the son of the owner of a successful sporting goods store where Newman worked briefly following his father's death in 1950. "I came from a family of retail people," he has said, "but I never understood the allure or the romance of business. People say, 'Isn't it wonderful that you pursued the theater?' I didn't pursue the theater; I was running away from the sporting goods business."

Newman made his debut on Broadway in *Picnic* in 1953 after attending the Yale School of Drama. Fifty-one years and seventy-one movies later, he has earned every honor Hollywood has to offer, the affection of everyone who knows him and the admiration of millions of adoring fans.

Among his many honors are ten nominations for an Academy Award, the first in 1958 for his role in *Cat on a Hot Tin Roof,* the last for his role in *The Road to Perdition* in 2003. He won an Oscar for Best Actor for his role in *The Color of Money* in 1985 and is one of the few actors to have received an Honorary Oscar for Career Achievement. In 1994 he was awarded the Jean Hersholt Humanitarian Award from the Academy of Motion Picture Arts and Sciences for his contributions to society.

Ironically, Newman's "contributions to society" have taken him back into the retail world he tried to escape. To hear him tell it, it began innocently enough.

In 1981, Newman, his wife Joanne Woodward and a friend, A. E. Hotchner, filled empty wine bottles with his homemade salad dressing so they could dispense them to friends and neighbors during the family's Christmas-carol outings. To his surprise, people started coming back for refills. That's when Newman's business instincts and his competitive juices kicked in. Since everybody seemed to love this stuff, he thought, maybe it would be fun to see if it would sell in local shops.

"The initial challenge," Newman says, "was to get someone to bottle it and put it up on the shelf to see whether it could compete with other people's products. From there things kept escalating."

Since then Newman's Own product line has escalated from salad dressings to pasta sauces, salsas, popcorn, lemonade and steak sauce. It has become, quite simply, a business phenomenon. The company has generated more than $1 billion in sales, with all of its profits going to charity.

In 1982, Newman gave away approximately $1 million. Since then, his company has donated over $150 million to charity. Hundreds of charities from schools for the deaf to theaters for low-income children to camps for kids with serious diseases and civil rights groups, have benefited.

In a world where companies that give away 2 percent of their profits to charity are considered generous, Newman's Own stands alone. It is the only company in the nation giving away every cent of its profits. "It's a way to use silliness for some good," Newman says. "The instant I decided this would be business, I realized that we really have to give all the money away.

"I am confounded by the stinginess of some institutions and some people," he explains. "You can only put away so much stuff in your closet. In 1987, the average CEO earned seventy times more than someone working in his factory. It's now 410 times. I don't think there is anything odd about philanthropy. It's the other stance that confounds me."

When asked if the success of his company has surprised him, he told one reporter, "I can only say that, if someone told me twenty years ago that I'd have my face on a bottle of salad dressing, I'd have got them committed. But it's turned out in a way that we've never, ever expected. The spaghetti sauce is now outgrossing my films, but I'm fighting back."

Newman's Own's motto is "Shameless Exploitation In Pursuit of the Common Good." That motto expresses Newman's wry sense of humor, but it also expresses an understanding that celebrity is a gift like so many others that only has meaning when put to good use.

In Newman's words, "From salad dressings all blessings flow."

★ ★ ★ ★

Mimi Silbert

Mimi Silbert has made an interesting observation. After thirty years of working with prison populations, Mimi says the chief characteristic of people in prison is that they are almost always on the receiving end.

"They are either receivers of punishment and hate and aggression or the receivers of welfare, charity or therapy," she says, "but they are never the doers. They are never the givers."

At their core, these people are the "takers" of the world—the takers of life and property, the takers of community services and assistance. They are "self" centered and "self" involved. They have never learned to look beyond their own immediate needs and interests. Some value their slightest desire more than another's life. But Mimi Silbert has shown they are not lost forever. She has helped turn around more than 20,000 hardened criminals, making productive citizens of former felons and drug addicts.

"Our average resident is violent, belongs to a gang and has eighteen felony convictions," Mimi Silbert says. "That means eighteen strikes in a country where three strikes puts you in prison for life. And we have never had an arrest. We have never had a crime committed in twenty-five years by these people."

Mimi's approach evolved out of her experience as a prison psychologist. It didn't take her long, she recalls, to decide that the system of institutionalization and punishment doesn't work.

"It's those of us who are givers who get to feel terrific about ourselves," Mimi said. "So it became clear to me, if I really was going to do something, it meant setting up an environment in which everybody is a giver and everybody is a doer, as well as a receiver and a learner."

From the beginning, Mimi's goal was to create a criminal rehabilitation center whose central tenet was self-sufficiency. She started out in a small San Francisco apartment. She worked with ex-cons and drug addicts, holding group counseling sessions and seeking training for them in employable skills. Everyone involved, including Silbert, pooled their incomes and shared resources.

Today, Delancey Street Foundation is housed on the San Francisco waterfront in a $30 million, three-acre complex called the Embarcadero Triangle. The complex, complete with apartments, shops, restaurants and theaters, was funded by an unsecured bank loan. It was built entirely by Silbert's extended brood of ex-cons. She personally supervised the job and acted as the project manager.

Silbert is the only nonresident employee of Delancey Street. The operation is staffed and run entirely by ex-cons. In all, Delancey Street has successfully developed and run twenty businesses that provide more than 60 percent of what it costs to run the organization. Among the business the residents operate are retail stores, a restaurant, a moving company and $1 million Christmas tree sale project.

In the process, Mimi has helped over 10,000 people receive their high school equivalency degrees. Over 1,000 of these students have gone on to graduate from vocational school. Thirty students have received their BA, and another twenty are in the process of earning their degrees at San Francisco State University.

Despite Delancey Street's phenomenal growth and success over the years, the basic tenets that Silbert began with remain constant: each resident must own up to self-responsibility, develop at least three marketable skills, perform volunteer work and serve as a role model for other residents. "Each one teach one" is the guiding principle of Delancey Street.

"We compare ourselves to Harvard," Mimi says. "Both are four-year programs. They take the top two percent and teach them everything they need to know to become successful. We take the bottom two percent of the population—we're equally snotty about our bottom two percent—and then we teach people who are used to being self-centered and full of hate to become full of love and to take care of each other.

"We give no therapy because the only therapy that works is to forget about yourself for a while and worry about somebody else," she concludes. "In the need to help someone else, all your strengths will emerge."

★ ★ ★ ★

Dr. Robert Pamplin Jr.

No one I know is more accomplished than Bob Pamplin Jr. No one I know is more driven to make appropriate use of his talents.

"God loaned me the ability to be successful," he says. "It is my duty to make good use of the capital he has provided."

The focus of Pamplin's life revolves around a determined effort to live up to his God-given potential. Pamplin holds eight degrees, has received countless honors and honorary degrees, and has had incredible financial success. He is a businessman, farmer, minister, philanthropist and the author of thirteen books, including two Book-of-the-Month Club selections. He is perennially listed by *Forbes* and *Fortune* magazines as one of the wealthiest men in America, having made his first million in the stock market as an undergraduate in the '60s.

Over the last decade, Pamplin has founded or purchased at least one new company a year, focusing on companies that manufacture and distribute the basics of daily living—food, wine, concrete, textiles, retail shops and entertainment. He is the president and CEO of the R. B. Pamplin Corporation, a family owned company with annual sales of more than $800 million.

He is also the founder of the *Portland Tribune* newspaper, Columbia Empire Farms, NorthWest retail stores and Pamplin Communications. Pamplin Communications is the parent company for Pamplin Broadcasting, Pamplin Entertainment, the Oregon Publication Corporation and Christian Supply Centers. Together, these companies encompass radio stations, record labels, video and live show entertainment, newspapers, and retail stores.

Ours is an age marked by the perfection of means and the obscurity of ends. We learn skills without considering their application, pursue power without purpose, gather possessions we will never need and resources we will never use. Pamplin is determined to put his abilities to their best use. As part of that effort, the R. B. Pamplin Corporation annually gives 10 percent of pretax profits to about 200 charities nationwide.

While all waste is an affront to God, the greatest waste is the waste of time and the waste of potential. While he was enormously successful in business, Pamplin came to understand God is more concerned with what you make of yourself than what you make in the world. Often, it comes down to the simple fact that why you do what you do is as important, if not more important, than what you do. This reality came into focus for Bob Pamplin when he was diagnosed with cancer at the age of thirty-three.

Two years later, he was in good health, starting a new company and wondering why he was spared. "Why me? Why was I saved?" he asked. The question remained open for months.

"Whenever I think back on the cancer," Bob says now, "it is clear that God has loved me enough to apply shock treatment to my soul. His direction for my life has come in jolts, always forcing me out of my naked dependence on self and back into humble trust in him."

His brush with cancer inspired Pamplin to enroll in a seminary. On graduation, he founded Christ Community Church and established a unique ministry of applied Christianity. Under Pamplin's direction, Christ Community Ministries serves more than sixty agencies in the greater Portland, Oregon, metropolitan area, feeding more than 1,000 people each day.

Pamplin's thousand-acre Columbia Empire Farms produces hazelnuts, strawberries, raspberries, marionberries, huckleberries and a vineyard. These products, as well as beef from Pamplin's 60,000 acre R2Ranch in eastern Oregon, are used to support Christ Community Ministries.

Pamplin is committed to helping members of society who are less fortunate, but in a creative way that allows individuals to become contributing partners in the society. He wants to make an investment in the total person.

"We are all important, no matter what our circumstances. It is really not the title or the material wealth that is the worth. It is the human being," Pamplin says. "Our lives aren't just surrounded by bricks and mortar and polished wood. It is the people who we come into contact with every day that give our lives character. It is the people who are the soul of our society, and for our soul to have any value whatsoever, we have to live by certain principles—traditions of family unity, service to others, caring, honor and fair dealing."

★ ★ ★ ★

Wally Amos

Wally Amos is a joyful man. He laughs a lot and takes an obvious delight in life. "I love my work," he says. "I love what I do. I love people. I love life."

His joy and love of life are reflected in the product that made him rich and famous and in the many good things he has chosen to do with his fortune and fame.

Like so many who go on to do well in business, Wally's began working at an early age, shining shoes and doing odd jobs as a boy in Tallahassee, Florida. At the age of twelve, his parents separated, and he went to live with his Aunt Della in Harlem.

"Aunt Della was the first person to make chocolate chip cookies for me," Amos remembers. "She was a very loving person. She gave me some tenderness and nourished that aspect of my personality."

At first, Wally thought he might be a cook. He enrolled in Food Trades High School, but dropped out his senior year to join the U.S. Air Force. While in the service, he earned a high school equivalency diploma that made him eligible to attend secretarial school after he was discharged.

After a series of jobs that required him to start at the bottom and work his way up, Amos was hired by the William Morris Talent Agency. Again, he started at the bottom, but he was so industrious that he was promoted and made an agent within a year. He recruited Simon and Garfunkel and worked with the Supremes, the Temptations and "nearly every other rock group that came along."

Seven years later, Amos left William Morris to start his own talent agency. When that business began to fail, he started looking for something else to do. He turned to the cookies that had come to symbolize the most positive aspects of his life.

For years, he had made chocolate chip cookies at home, giving them to friends, and leaving them behind as his calling card. With the help of Helen Reddy, Marvin Gaye, Bill Cosby and a few other friends Amos made a leap of faith and opened his first chocolate chip shop in March 1975. He decided to do what he loved, what felt good, even if it wasn't a huge success. With that expectation, he opened a small cookie store. It was the first shop in the world to sell nothing but chocolate chip cookies.

Amos had chased fame and fortune for years. When he stopped, it found him. The store was an immediate success. The first year, Wally grossed $300,000. He had christened himself "Famous Amos" before the shop opened, but soon a number of other names were born in the press, including "the King of Cookies," "Father of the Gourmet Cookie" and the "Face that Launched a Thousand Chips."

After two years in business, Famous Amos was grossing $1 million. In 1979, he made $4 million; in 1980, $5 million. Public surveys defined him as one of the most recognizable people in the United States. He promoted his image with such success that his trademark embroidered shirt and Panama hat now reside in the Smithsonian National Museum of American History.

A *Time* magazine cover story called him one of the "hot new rich." *Newsweek* profiled him as the "the progenitor of the upscale cookie," calling him "the greatest cookie salesman alive." At its apex, *Time* estimated the Famous Amos empire to be a $250 million-a-year designer-cookie industry. Wally was producing 3.5 tons of handmade, fresh-baked cookies a day.

But in 1985, the cookie began to crumble. "I forgot to put a good management team under the flying carpet," Wally says. Before long investors had begun chipping away at his stake in

Famous Amos Cookies, diminishing his control. Three years later, Famous Amos was sold, and Wally Amos left the company he started without a dime. Not only that, he lost the right to use his name and likeness in any food-related business, because these things were so intimately identified with Famous Amos Chocolate Chip Cookies.

"Making chocolate chip cookies made me 'Famous.' Losing the company that made my name a household word made me wonder if life would ever be the same again. Despite my missteps in business, I found that my life got better and I got stronger," Wally said. "The company hadn't failed me. I failed it."

Two years later, when Wally decided to start another company, his former partners replied by suing him. They sought an injunction, forcing him to shut down and telling him he would never be allowed to use his legal name in any other business venture.

Most of us would have been more than a little upset, but Wally responded differently. "I did not stop living my life for one single moment," he said. "I refused to be reduced and defeated."

Wally responded by starting yet another venture selling gourmet muffins. Since he couldn't use his own name, he called this one The Uncle Noname Cookie Company. In 1999, The Uncle Noname Cookie Company was merged into Uncle Wally's, Inc., allowing Wally to expand his product line.

As part of that effort, Wally has returned to the thing he loves. He re-entered the chocolate chip cookie business with the introduction of Aunt Della's Chocolate Chip Cookies, named after the woman who inspired him and shaped the direction of his life. Uncle Wally's is now growing at the rate of 35 percent a year with products sold in 3,500 stores nationwide.

Along the way, Wally Amos says he has gained a larger, personal victory.

"If I look back on my whole life, it is as if I have always

been in training," Wally muses. "It is as if every move I made was preparing me for something else. My journey has taken me on some very unusual paths. I have shined shoes, sold newspapers, delivered groceries, cooked in restaurants, worked as a secretary, served in the Air Force and worked at Saks Fifth Avenue, which led to show business and then the cookie business.

"It shows me how God shapes your life. On my best day, I couldn't have planned it. On my very best day, I couldn't have put the pieces together. I have come to believe the experiences you are having today have nothing to do with today. They are preparing you for your future."

★ ★ ★ ★

Nick Walters

As a fifth grader watching a commercial on lung disease during summer vacation, Nick Walters thought how lucky he was that he did not have any health problems. Less than a week later, Nick was hospitalized by the onset of juvenile diabetes. His blood sugar level was so high that it almost proved fatal.

When his condition stabilized, the doctors explained that his juvenile diabetes could be managed if he followed guidelines on diet and insulin. Eventually, they said, a cure would be found and the disease would no longer exist. It was only a matter of time and money.

Nick understood he had no control over time, but felt he could do something to help raise money. He set his goal, developed his business plan and got to work. He made presentations at health fairs, offices, schools and United Way meetings. He signed up his friends for JD Walk-A-Thons and involved his school in a myriad of fundraising activities.

By the time he had graduated from high school, Nick had raised three quarters of a million dollars for juvenile diabetes research. By the time he graduated from college, the total was at $1 million. Now after fourteen years of fund-raising, Nick has raised more than $2 million for The Juvenile Diabetes Research Foundation. He is one of the top fundraisers in the state of Maryland and the only person of his age to have passed the $2 million mark.

Nick's focus at the moment is on real estate—buying, selling and rehabilitating run-down properties in the inner city of Baltimore. He already has three rental units and is well on his way to his next million. All he has to do is what comes naturally.

"Enterprise to me is simply seeing a need and filling it," Nick says. "It doesn't matter whether it is business or charity. It takes a certain confidence because you are doing something that hasn't been done before, but it is not really that complicated. Whether it is a new activity, a new company, or an improvement in something that exists, if you believe in yourself you take it upon yourself to get it done. You believe first, then you get others to believe."

Ten

SPIRITUALITY

★ ★ ★ ★

Our constitution was designed only for a moral and religious people. It is wholly inadequate for the government of any other.

John Adams

★ ★ ★ ★

few years ago, I helped bring a matched pair of children from the Middle East to Give Kids the World in Orlando, Florida. Eight-year-old Maataz Kishta came from the Palestine. Nine-year-old Chaim Salinas was from Israel. Both boys were fighting cancer. Both had undergone a bone marrow transfer. Both faced long odds and were looking for a common miracle.

I met them at the airport in New York City. Almost by design, they seemed to come from different ends of the plane. Chaim, who must have been sitting up front, arrived first. Maataz came a few minutes later. They took positions on opposite sides of me while my translator helped me greet the children and their escorts.

While we waited for the plane to Orlando, they kept as much distance between themselves as possible. Both wanted to know what we had planned for them, but each asked their questions independently. There was no direct communication. They could not avoid being close from time to time, but there was no connection between them.

A week later, after playing together, eating together, sharing rides and experiencing the wonders of Orlando's theme parks, they left as friends. Somehow along the way, they learned they had more than a disease and a desire to meet Mickey Mouse in common. They realized all they both really wanted is what all children want—the right to enjoy life and grow up in peace.

"We are from different sides of the world," Chaim's mother, Shula, told Antonio Mora of *ABC News*, "but we hope people can learn from this. I know I have."

Maataz's father, Aatef, agreed, saying, "This is the most beautiful thing."

Man was created in God's image. Too often, we are inclined to return the favor, limiting God to our own likeness. Whether we are engaged in a national war or at a local high school football game, we pray for victory and hope to prevail, even though we know that there are an equal number of prayers on the other side, that both cannot win, and that our victory would devastate our opponent.

Some of us are so sure of our righteousness that we are bold enough to pray outright for the devastation of our enemies. Others take it upon themselves to correct God's mistakes and "cleanse" the world of all who do not share their passions or beliefs.

No matter how great and grave the differences between us may appear, below and above all is the eternal fact of brotherhood. If we believe there is one God, if we believe he is the Father of us all, then no child of God can be said to be outside the pale of human kinship, and no individual can be considered less human than any other.

For Alexis de Tocqueville, this spiritual base and the desire for religious freedom was the "point of departure" for the entire American experience. "It must never be forgotten that religion gave birth to Anglo-American society," he said.

The Founding Fathers were deeply religious. Thomas Jefferson, who some say was among the least devout, had 190 religious books in his library. The Declaration of Independence he drafted speaks of inalienable rights endowed to man by our Creator.

On the back side of the Great Seal of the United States, which Jefferson helped design along with Franklin and Adams, is a pyramid with an eye and the words "*Annuit Koeptis.*" Those words translated from the Latin mean "He has favored our undertakings." He, of course, is God. The phrase refers to the Founding Fathers' belief that God favored our nation and provided for our success during America's struggle for freedom. During the Revolutionary War, prayer was held daily in the halls of the Continental Congress. To this day, that tradition continues. Every session of Congress opens with a prayer.

George Washington in his first inaugural address — the first inaugural address of a freely elected leader of a democratic nation in the history of the world — made clear his devotion to a higher power and his belief that God controlled America's destiny.

"No people can be bound to acknowledge and adore the invisible hand which conducts the affairs of men more than those of the United States," he said. "Every step by which they have advanced to the character of an independent nation seems to have been distinguished by some token of providential agency."

To de Tocqueville the significance of this relation was as much practical as it was spiritual. He saw the faith of our fathers and the institutionalization of their beliefs in our democracy as part of the genius of America, tempering and balancing the values of ambition and enterprise.

"It must be acknowledged that equality, which brings great benefits to the world, nevertheless suggests to men some very dangerous propensities," he said. "It tends to isolate them from each other, to concentrate every man's attention upon himself; and it lays open the soul to an inordinate love of material gratification. The greatest advantage of religion is to inspire diametrically contrary principles.

"The taste for well-being is the prominent and indelible feature of democratic times," he continued. "The chief concern of religion is to purify, to regulate and to restrain the excessive and exclusive taste for well-being which men feel at periods of equality."

George Washington clearly agreed. "Of all the dispositions and habits, which lead to political prosperity, religion and morality are indispensable supports," he wrote. "Reason and experience both forbid us to expect that national morality can prevail in exclusion of religious principle."

Every president since Washington has come from a similar place of faith. In the words of President Harry Truman, "The American people stand firm in the faith which has inspired this Nation from the beginning. We believe that all men have a right to equal justice under law and equal opportunity to share the common good. We believe that all men have a right to freedom of thought and expression. We believe that all men are created equal because they are created in the image of God. From this faith we will not be moved."

Even Calvin Coolidge, known for saying little, had something to say on this subject. He said, "Our doctrine of equality and liberty and humanity comes from our belief in the brotherhood of man through the fatherhood of God. We do not need more national development, we need more spiritual development. We do not need more intellectual power, we need more spiritual power. We do not need more knowledge, we need more character. We do not need more law, we need more religion. We do not need more of the things that are seen, we need more of the things that are unseen."

Whether or not you believe America came from God, it is clear the values that shaped our democracy were founded on religious principles and, in particular, the Christian way of life. While it has become less fashionable to talk about the role of religion in public life, its influence is constant and undeniable.

The number of religions practiced in the United States now embraces all the known religions of the world, but these differing paths to the same end only serve to reinforce the same fundamental fact: America is still one nation, under God. In survey after survey, in overwhelming majorities, Americans say they believe in God. In two of the most recent surveys, more than nine out of ten Americans—95 percent—told *ABC News* polltakers they believed in God. A Gallup survey found nearly the same thing. Nearly nine out of ten—86 percent—told Gallup they believed in God, while another 8 percent said they believe in some form of a "universal spirit or higher power."

Like our founding fathers, many people, including those profiled in the section that follows, look for opportunities to express their faith in their daily lives.

S. Truett Cathy, the founder of Chick-fil-A, takes his faith so seriously he closes shop every Sunday—to the surprise and consternation of his competitors in the fast food industry. "If I have to work seven days a week to succeed in the restaurant business," Cathy says, "I'm in the wrong business." The remarkable success of his company proves he is not, and he doesn't.

Bill Shore has raised hundreds of millions of dollars to fight hunger, motivated by what he believes to be a distillation of the Golden Rule. "If you learn how to be a good neighbor and to serve others and be good to the people around you," he says, "you'll know the major principles of every religion in the world."

Katy Ballenger, a former Miss Teen USA, set out to change the world at an early age. She was surprised to find it changed her.

Tom Chappell, founder of Tom's of Maine, created a new concept he calls "compassionate capitalism" to allow him to use his company's success for the greater good, while John Fling, the "Saint of South Carolina," has for forty-five years done whatever needs doing for an extended family that includes hundreds of children, seniors, disabled and blind people.

These five people exemplify the deep sense of spirituality that animates our lives and feeds the well of goodness at the heart of America.

★ ★ ★ ★

S. Truett Cathy grew up during the Depression. His father tried to support his family of seven without success during those hard times, farming, repairing cars and selling insurance. To help make ends meet, his mother began taking borders into the house the family rented on the east side of Atlanta, but things still remained tight.

When he was eight years old, Truett decided it was time for him to start contributing. He began selling Coca-Cola door to door. He is enough of a businessman to still remember that he made a nickel profit on each half dozen Cokes he sold. Later, he began buying Cokes by the case—twenty-four for eighty cents—doubling his profit.

"I thought that was big business," Truett told me the first time we met.

Next he sold magazine subscriptions to the *Ladies' Home Journal* and *Saturday Evening Post* door to door. He also delivered newspapers and sold peanuts in the stands during Georgia Tech football games. But despite his best efforts, the family fell further and further into debt.

Truett's ability to help was interrupted when he was drafted during World War II. But after the war, he had enough of a grubstake to think about starting a business. He decided to buy a restaurant with his brother. It was so tiny they called it the Dwarf House. The brothers put in $4,000 of their own money and borrowed $6,000 more.

"We couldn't afford to fail," Truett says, "because that was everything we had."

While they were totally committed to financial success,

Truett and his brother were not willing to abandon their principles. They had attended church and Sunday school all their lives and were not about to stop just because they owned a restaurant.

"Our decision to close on Sunday was our way of honoring God and directing our attention to things more important than our business," Truett says. "If it took seven days a week to make a living with a restaurant, then we needed to be in some other line of work."

Through the years, Truett has never wavered from that fundamental belief. Today, that one small restaurant has evolved into a chain of restaurants known as Chick-fil-A, a billion dollar, privately owned company with more than 1,000 franchise outlets in thirty-nine states. Despite the loss of revenue from closing on what is one of the most profitable days of the week for his competitors, Chick-fil-A units have higher sales per square foot than McDonalds, Wendy's, Burger King and all the rest.

In 1982, Truett was tested when Chick-fil-A experienced its first and only decrease in sales for existing stores. Two of Chick-fil-A's competitors, Wendy's and McDonald's, had finally decided to add chicken to their menus, driving up the cost and cutting into the market. Complicating this scenario was the fact that interest rates were at an all-time high—21 percent—increasing the cost of borrowing and inhibiting the construction of new outlets.

In October of that year, Truett scheduled a two-day executive committee meeting to review where they were and decide what to do. Things were as bad as they had ever been. "I think I expected us go to the mountains and come back with a blueprint for success," Truett says.

Instead, the committee quickly decided they were operating the company prudently and responsibly, dismissing current problems as a reflection of the larger problems in the economy at that time. Rather than fix what wasn't broken, they found themselves asking a more fundamental questions: Why are we in business? Why are we here? Why are we alive? "The discussion quickly focused on our individual priorities," Truett recalls. "We were unanimous in our belief that each of us wanted to glorify God in all we say and do. It was only natural that we would also want to glorify God through our work."

By the end of the day, Cathy's team had developed two statements that have become Chick-fil-A's corporate purpose: *"To glorify God by being a faithful steward of all that is entrusted to us and to have a positive influence on all whom come in contact with Chick-fil-A."* The following year, without any structural change in operations, Chick-fil-A experienced a 28.9 percent increase in company sales.

"When we established our corporate purpose," Truett explains, "I gave Chick-fil-A to God. I operate it and take care of it along with our staff and operators, but it is his business. When I remember that, I have a totally different feeling about what we are doing."

As part of their charge to have a positive influence on everyone they come in contact with, Chick-fil-A operators take special care in selecting the teenagers who work in their restaurants and try to model positive character traits for them. As an example, Truett tells the story of seeing a young man who worked for him smoking a cigarette in the kitchen. Disturbed by this self-destructive act, Truett told him he was developing a terrible habit. The young man responded by saying he was buying cigarettes from a machine in the store. Truett was making a profit, so what did he care?

Truett had to admit the young man was right. He was making more profit per square foot from the space the cigarette machine occupied than any other square foot in the restaurant. Nevertheless, the next morning he called the cigarette company and asked them to take it out.

Chick-fil-A gives away more than $1 million a year in

college scholarships to employees, but the company's contribution to young people goes far beyond its employees. The company supports eleven foster care homes, runs summer camps and invests millions of dollars in character-building programs for children.

"My riches are my family and my foster children," Truett explains. "I try to store my material wealth in my hands, not my heart, so that I always feel free to give it away when the opportunity arises. I pray for discernment to know when and how to give.

"You cannot be a success in life unless you develop a heart for other people," Truett concludes. "I say to my wife often times, we are not in the chicken business, we are in the people business. It is each and every one of our responsibilities to use what resources we have to help other people."

★ ★ ★ ★

Bill Shore

"The fundamental idea for Share Our Strength—that everybody has a strength to share—is very spiritual," Bill Shore says. "Everybody's been given a gift of some type, and if we can tap into that, if we can create vehicles in which people can contribute whatever their particular unique talent or gift is, then that can really change the world."

Twenty years ago, Shore was a top Congressional aide with some thirteen years of experience at the highest levels of government. He was involved in a presidential campaign when he read a small article on the front page of the *Washington Post.* The headline said 200,000 people would die that summer of starvation in Ethiopia. Most disturbing was the fact that the story was written in the future tense, as if the calamity could not be avoided. The experts saw it coming, but said there was nothing they could do about it.

"I was shocked," Shore recalls. "To me the newspaper story read like an invitation to act."

Shore responded by founding Share Our Strength (SOS). The mission of SOS is to alleviate and prevent hunger by distributing grants, educating the public and organizing community outreach programs. "Billy Shore gave it all up to fight hunger," the *Washington Post* reported. "Is this guy for real?"

To a cynical press, it seemed improbable. But SOS has since become one of the nation's largest private, nonprofit source of funds for antihunger efforts. SOS takes no money from government and relatively little from foundations, but it has made grants to 1,000 organizations, helping the 33 million Americans who cannot get through the month without food aid. In all, Bill Shore and Share our Strength have raised more than $100 million to help people who don't have enough to eat.

The key to Shore's success was his discovery that people who might not want to write a check for a good cause will often respond generously if you ask them to share their skill, to donate work they're good at doing. It began when Shore recruited 8,000 chefs to do for hunger what they do best—cook. "It's a classic win-win-win situation. The chefs get good visibility and an opportunity to be part of the community. People who come get great value for their dollar. And our sponsors underwrite the costs not only because they want to be good corporate citizens, but also to build relationships with their customers, who are the chefs. We raise about $5 million a year from Taste of the Nation, 100 percent of which is donated."

In 1993 American Express and Share Our Strength launched the Charge Against Hunger—one of the largest corporate commitments ever made to hunger relief in the United States. American Express agreed to give three cents to SOS every time someone used its credit card. That deal brought SOS $22.5 million.

"We try to be a financial engine for a lot of the rest of the hunger relief community," Bill says. "We can identify new ways to create financial revenues for their efforts. A lot of what we did in SOS when we first began, and even now, consists of getting people who typically don't consider themselves activists or politically active involved in an issue in a very special way—by connecting it to their own skills, their talents."

As one small example of the impact of Shore's approach, 400,000 children have been added to the school breakfast programs because of SOS's efforts, and another 200,000 children participate in summer feeding programs. Impressive as that is, Shore says he learned on Capitol Hill that when it comes to helping the poor, money is not enough.

"It takes mentoring. It takes working with people. It takes coaching," Shore says. "It takes that type of personal exchange to really turn someone's life around."

When you ask him what motivates him, he says his parents were nonobservant Jews who did not think he should be bar mitzvahed. "I lived in a very Jewish neighborhood and that was borderline scandalous at the time," Shore recalls. "But they offered me this explanation. They said, 'We are going to teach you to be a good neighbor and to serve others, and if you understand both of those things . . . you'll know the major principles of every religion in the world.

"That didn't connect immediately, but I have thought a lot about it since. I have come to believe that being in touch with yourself and what gifts you were given, trying to understand where they came from and what opportunities you have to use and nurture them, is a very spiritual experience. A state of grace exists when who you are to the world is who you really are inside. Being in touch with your strengths and your gifts gets you pretty close to that."

Remembering his days at the Senate, Shore knows there's always a temptation to think about the responsibility other people have for solving problems. "But to accomplish change on a really large scale," he says, "we are going to have to look more at ourselves. People are going to have to find a whole new way to think about themselves, their responsibilities to their neighbors and their communities. I would love to believe SOS has played some small role in creating a climate in which that type of moral leadership can emerge."

★ ★ ★ ★

Katy Ballenger

At the age of fifteen, Katy Ballenger started volunteering at Primary Children's Medical Center in Salt Lake City, Utah. She had no idea it would change her life forever.

On her last day volunteering at the hospital, the nurses introduced her to a two-year-old terminally ill boy named Joshua. Joshua spoke little and smiled less. He was depressed and unresponsive.

Katy read stories to him and played with him all day, trying her best to entertain him and cheer him up. Finally, she broke through and the boy laughed. He clung to her when it was time to leave and said he was sad to see her go. As she walked out the door, Katy says, "I realized I had made a difference in this child's life."

She was hooked. Katy began looking for other volunteer experiences and soon dreamed of sharing the rewards of service with her friends.

"The most important thing we can do for ourselves is to help someone else," Katy says. "Through service, barriers are broken, friendships are created, and horizons are expanded. When we help others to be happy, we find happiness ourselves. Volunteering does just as much for the people giving the service as it does for the people receiving it."

To accomplish her goal, Katy, then an A student at Olympus High School, founded H.U.G.S. (Help Us Give Service) Club, an organization linking student volunteers to community needs. She began by identifying more than 150 different agencies in the Salt Lake City area that could use student volunteers and began organizing service opportunities.

"What's involved in giving a hug?" Katy asks in explaining the club's name. "The first thing is putting your arms around someone. It's showing someone you care, even if sometimes it means stepping outside your comfort zone. The best thing about a hug is that it works two ways! The person giving the hug benefits just as much as the person receiving the hug. In other words, it's a lot like service."

In the first year, Katy succeeded in involving 123 students who gave more than 2,200 hours of service to the Utah Food Bank, the March of Dimes, Habitat for Humanity and other community agencies. The club puts on "unbirthday parties" for homeless children who didn't get to celebrate their birthdays during the year, takes pets to rest homes so the residents can have company and raises money for charitable organizations.

Under her leadership, HUGS has grown into a statewide, nationwide and eventually international service organization. Though HUGS started small, there are now HUGS chapters from Alaska to Australia.

In the last three years of high school, Katy rendered 4,500 hours of volunteer service. She continued in college, volunteering with Special Olympics, working with the Brigham Young University service association, serving as a Big Sister, participating in programs for inner city girls and serving as treasurer of the Utah Commission of Volunteers. She also worked with the President's Summit for America's Future, which launched America's Promise and was featured in *Time, National Geographic, Newsweek, U. S. News* and *People.*

In 1997, when she won the Miss Teen America title, she decided to take full advantage of the opportunity and become a missionary for service. During the following year, she had an opportunity to travel across the United States and Australia. Everywhere she went, she spoke about the value of volunteering.

Katy, a devout Mormon, feels HUGS club was divinely

inspired. "I knew it was from Heavenly Father," she says. "The best way to leave your mark is to leave your fingerprint on the soul of another individual. That's my life philosophy." And that also means following Christ's example everyday. "Mormons really live our religion," Katy explains. "If I want to follow Christ, really follow him, I must serve."

★ ★ ★ ★

Tom Chappell

Religion and business have always been part of Tom Chappell's life. As a boy, he posed for the Norman Rockwell painting *The Choirboy.* The painting wound up on the cover of the *Saturday Evening Post* in 1954. His entrepreneurial spirit came from his father who started his own textile business, teaching him about the corporate world and living with risk.

"My father was always in his own business," Chappell recalls. "I understand the struggle of sustaining a small business because I sat at the dinner table every night and heard about the realities of whether or not you are going to stay in business or how you solve a tough ethical dilemma. At the same time, religion has always played an important part in my life."

During his college years, his father's business fell on hard times, and Tom was forced to leave school to work to raise the funds he needed to finish. He finally graduated from Trinity College in Hartford in 1966 and went to work for the Aetna Insurance Company It didn't take him long to become disenchanted with corporate culture.

"I discovered in working for a large company that I really needed to have the freedom and flexibility to be self-expressive," he says. "I needed to be creative about bringing good product ideas into business."

Two years later, at the age of twenty-eight, Chappell was ready to launch his own company. He knew phosphates were polluting our lakes and streams so he borrowed $5,000 from a friend and set about developing a nonpolluting, nonphosphate cleaning compound for the dairy farms around Kennebunk, Maine.

"During the first year of our business," he says, "that's all we sold."

From the beginning, Chappell was interested in a different kind of company. "Business had to have a slightly different quality about it for me," he explains, "because I wasn't interested in just making money. That's certainly a requirement, but money was never the driving force." The driving force was Chappell's desire to see if business can be accountable to the aims of society and be profitable at the same time.

In the second year of his business, Chappell added a phosphate-free laundry detergent to his product line. Over the next few years, he expanded to personal products, riding the growing tide of environmental concern and interest in all-natural products. In 1975, the company, Tom's of Maine, produced the first natural toothpaste with fluoride and developed the first natural baby shampoo.

Over the years, Tom's of Maine all-natural products found wider and wider acceptance. The company grew at a five-year compounded growth rate of 20 percent and soon went national. Today, Tom's of Maine is the leading producer of natural personal products and one of the most successful small corporations in America.

But despite his success, Tom felt there was something missing. "I didn't like what success felt like," he said. "I felt empty. I wanted to know what was wrong."

In 1986, he turned back to the church that had been so much a part of his formative life. After talking with his spiritual advisors, many of whom were now in their 80s and had known him all his life, Tom found himself enrolling in Harvard Divinity School.

"As a young person growing up in the church, what do you learn? Be kind, be caring, be decent," Tom says. "But it wasn't until I got to Harvard that I could make a study of this and say, 'Look, these inclinations, these orientations to be good are normal. They have been an issue for religious groups for the last 3,000 years of civilization. Whether you are a Buddhist, Taoist, Jew, Christian or Muslim, they all come up with a way of speaking about the reality of getting through life with meaning. . . . The way to meaning is to do things for others.'"

During the four years he sat in the lecture halls at Harvard Divinity School pursing his masters degree, one thought kept recurring: Could he stick to his respect for humanity and nature and still make a successful company even more successful? He found the answers in the writings of the great philosophers Immanuel Kant, Jonathan Edwards and Martin Buber.

In the *Soul of Business,* Chappell writes, "They clarified for me that: you don't have to sell your soul to make your numbers, nor do you have to give up good sound business practices to allow your values to participate in even the smallest, most pragmatic business decision. Suddenly, I entertained the possibility that I could actually find a way to manage for profit *and* for the common good."

Chappell coined the term "Common Good Capitalism" to describe his new way of doing business. In his mind, Common Good Capitalism integrates aggressive competition with intentional pursuit of goodness. Doing good is seen as an opportunity not a duty.

"Business is about both the world of incentives and the world of love," he explains. "When you act out of love and concern for the well-being of your customers and the people who work for you, you get the best of everything.

"We as growing people need to be more committed to becoming more knowing. We need to be willing to learn at whatever age, because life is a lifelong process of learning and growing and figuring out how to live right. We need more than the Constitution to tell us this. We need a national mission statement for America, and that national mission statement needs to have something to say about the importance of being informed and being responsible.

"With the freedoms that we were granted, we are expected

to figure out how to bring society along, how to bring the family along, how to bring communities along, how to bring company cultures along, how to bring God's creation along.

"I'm not asking people to give up their private aims," he concludes. "I am asking them to put their private aims in some kind of accountability to society aims. That is how I see business—as an enterprise granted by our free society to function and deliver services and products at a profit. Given that, we have to go about that enterprise in a way that does not deteriorate human dignity, environmental sacredness, animals and so forth. You have to bring it all along.

"The mystery and paradox of life is that we live in the skin called 'me.' We think we are a self-sufficient organism, but the spirit runs out of the skin, goes beyond the skin, and finds relation with the spirit of another. It is in discovering the spirit that we discover the meaning of life."

★ ★ ★ ★

John Fling grew up dirt-poor, one of seventeen children raised on the banks of the Chattahoochee River. "We weren't sharecroppers," he said. "We were sharecroppers' helpers. There wasn't much that we ate that we didn't catch out of the water, dig out of the ground or shake out of a tree."

When he was old enough to strike out on his own, John got a job supervising children selling newspapers in Columbia, South Carolina. He was surprised to find many of these children were growing up the same way he had.

"When you have seventy-five to 100 children with you all day long," John said, "you are going to know where they live and what they need." He began helping out by taking money out of his pocket to buy hungry children something to eat.

When I met John twenty-five years later he was still driving a truck, but his spontaneous acts of compassion had evolved into caring for an extended family that included 400 children, forty blind people, and over 100 seniors. What John did for them was nothing more nor less than most of us do for our own families. He checked on their well-being, transported them to medical appointments when necessary, bought them food, kept them company and responded to their specific needs.

"When the phone rings, you never know what is on it," he says. Ninety-five percent of his calls are people in need. Whatever is needed, he tries to supply.

John has never asked anyone to share his load, passed the hat or held a fund-raiser. His approach is simple. He just gives away whatever he has. For more than forty-five years, he has given away everything he has been given and nearly everything he has earned.

John doesn't have a TV, though he has given dozens to others. He doesn't own a home, but he has helped others buy and keep their own homes. The clothes he gives away are often better than the clothes he wears. After a lifetime of work, all he has to his name is enough money to bury whoever dies first—himself or his wife. "It don't matter about who dies second," he says.

Fling helps the elderly with the medicine they need, pays the rent when cash is short or helps with the utility bills. "If the refrigerator or the air conditioning goes out," he says, "that's a real problem because old people suffer in this heat, and if a refrigerator goes out they are in trouble.

"The blind people like to get out," Fling says. He takes them to the beach or out to the lake to go fishing.

Children emerge magically at the sound of his truck as he drives through the city. At each stop, his response is the same. First, he embraces as many children as he can hold and asks them how they are and what they need, digging into his pocket to give them money for food, clothing or school supplies. "But love is what they need most," he says. "These children need love more than they need money."

Fling is unincorporated and refuses to form an organization. There is no board to direct him, no committee to support his activities. "I don't ever ask for anything," he says. "I don't do anything to promote my activities. If somebody wants to help me, I will accept it but I don't ask for it. My billfold is a lot of times empty, but when I've got it, I use it."

Every Sunday, Fling gets up at 5:30 A.M. to go to church. The church is next door but it takes him three hours to get there. He starts driving at 6:30 A.M., covering a fifty-five mile circuit, collecting children as he goes.

Forty-two children later he arrives at church, only to begin the return leg an hour later, stopping for lunch along the way. "It will be 2:30 P.M. before the kids get home, and many of them don't get no breakfast," he says.

While every child is treated like family by John Fling, sometimes the relationship is even closer. In 1951, John accompanied the police to settle a domestic dispute. The police officer explained the wife had been unfaithful. She had become pregnant and delivered a baby fathered by someone other than her husband. The infant's presence seemed to inflame the man, serving as a reminder of her infidelity. The couple argued all the time. This was the third police call to the same location in as many months.

After the police calmed the couple down, John asked if it would solve their problem with each other if he took the baby. When the couple readily agreed, John asked them to sign a paper giving him rights to the baby. He took the infant home and raised him as his son.

John Fling doesn't have much, but he has everything. His education is limited—he only made it through the third grade—but he is wise. He has never made a lot of money, but few people are as rich. He has never sought public acclaim, but few people are as well respected in his community.

"The really great men on earth are never known by their titled names, or seldom so," Harry Tippet said. "So significant has been their service, so distinguished their gifts, that their simple name is enough."

When you talk to the people of Columbia, South Carolina, you know John Fling has made it. People speak his name with reverence. Newspapers call him "a good Samaritan," "a good neighbor" or "the everyday Santa." But what most people call him is the "Saint of South Carolina."

Conclusion

Whatever America hopes to bring to pass in the world must first happen in the heart of America.

Dwight D. Eisenhower

Charles Carroll was the last surviving signatory of the Declaration of Independence, outliving Jefferson and Adams by six years. He was also the only Roman Catholic to sign the Declaration and, perhaps, the man who had the most to lose by doing so. Carroll was the wealthiest man in the colonies at the beginning of the Revolution with a fortune estimated at $2 million—a fortune worth hundreds of millions of dollars in today's terms. He could have stayed on the sidelines and lived comfortably, but he risked his wealth, as well as his life, for freedom.

Carroll had the satisfaction of living to see the fiftieth year of American independence. He died shortly thereafter, leaving us with these words:

"I do now here recommend to the present and future generations the principles of that important document as the best earthly inheritance their ancestors could bequeath to them, and pray that the civil and religious liberties they have secured in my country may be perpetuated to the remotest posterity and extend to the whole family of man!"

Our founder's promise and Carroll's bequest have materialized into the greatest nation the world has ever seen. The principles they established have brought us from thirteen obscure colonies to the world's only superpower. They have established new standards of life, liberty and happiness. Free men and those yearning to be free still look to the United States as the light of the world and the best hope for the future of mankind.

At the same time, many believe we are failing to live up to our own ideals. During a soccer elimination match in Mexico for the 2004 Olympics, fans whistled and booed when our national anthem was played. At various other times during the game, spontaneous chants of "Osama, Osama" were clearly heard.

In 2003, the European Commission sponsored a survey to see "What the World Thinks of America." Sixty-five percent of those polled throughout the world described America as arrogant; 33 percent said we were antagonistic. Only 23 percent of those surveyed thought our economic policies should be copied. An even smaller number—18 percent—spoke favorably of our popular culture.

Less than 20 percent of all Americans have a passport; an even smaller percentage of people in the rest of the world has visited our country. Most of what we know of the rest of the world and what they know of us comes from the media. With this understanding, the State Department convened a meeting shortly after September 11, 2001, to develop a strategy to address the growing tide of anti-Americanism. One of the conveners of the meeting suggested the best way to address the apparent misconception of America was to broadcast old movies like "It's a Wonderful Life" to show those in doubt what we are really like.

Tim Love, vice chairman of a leading advertising agency, was among those present. Surprised by this suggestion, he responded by asking what good that could possibly do. In an age when every program we see here is instantly available anywhere else in the world, a public relations effort of this kind only invites an inevitable comparison between what we are, what we think we are and what we would like to be.

President Eisenhower said, "Whatever America hopes to bring to pass in the world must first happen in the heart of America." It follows that whatever change is to come to pass in America—and in the world's perception of America—must first happen in the hearts of its people.

Values are not hereditary. Great ideals do not live in the hearts and minds of men simply because they are right. They must be taught. They must be learned and lived.

Most people want to have what we have. America and the world would be better served if we lived our lives so they want to be what we are. America's greatest export has always been our values. We have to be the change we want to see in the world.

Every little deed counts. For all of our failings—and we must admit there are some—there is redemption in the fact that no man can be faithful, honest and true without the world being better for it. Even the humblest among us can, by sheer act of will, help make America great and the world a better place.

Ultimately, human progress depends not so much on science and technology as it does on conscience and compassion. Peace is not God's gift to us. It is our gift to each other. Peace between nations cannot exist without love between individuals.

At the birth of our nation, a citizen approached Benjamin

Franklin and asked, "What kind of government have you given us?"

"A republic," Franklin replied, "if you can keep it."

The Republic will endure as long as we continue to cherish the ideals of the men who created it. From Bunker Hill to Berlin, the best of our blood have fought to defend democracy. But that is not enough. The battle for freedom is not reserved for the few or the brave. The battle for democracy must be fought here, as well as there, day by day, with the knowledge that liberty won today may be lost tomorrow.

"There is a new America every morning when we wake," Adlai Stevenson said, "and that new America is the sum of many small changes." Our task is to guide these changes and decide what kind of America we want it to be.

"Every year millions of Americans come to Washington to visit our national shrines—the Lincoln Memorial, the Washington Monument, the Capitol," former Secretary John Gardner said. "But the spirit of the nation does not reside in these physical structures. It is in the minds of the citizens who come to look at the structures. That is where a vital society begins; and, if it ends, that is where it will end."

If we lose faith, if we stop believing, if we become complacent and content with where we are and what we have, if we stop caring and trying to make things better, if we waver in our commitment to equality, liberty and justice, the monuments of our nation will become meaningless, and the dream that is known as America will disappear.

You and people like you, the people in this book, make our country great. The sprit of America is strengthened with every act of individual achievement, every word spoken for freedom, every vote cast in an election and every extension of liberty. The soul of America is nourished with every act of courage, kindness and compassion.

"We the people." We *are* the people. The story of America is our story. America will be whatever we are.

About The Heart of America

More . . .

If you know someone you think exemplifies America's core values, please tell us about them. We would love to hear their story. You may send a written description of this individual, a newspaper article or any other information that you think may be helpful to this address:

The Heart of America Foundation, 401 "F" Street, NW, Suite 325, Washington, DC 20001.

... About The Heart of America Foundation®

The Heart of America Foundation® was created to teach the values at the heart of America. We are nonsectarian, non-profit and nonpartisan. Believing with Albert Schweitzer that example isn't the best way to teach, it is the only way, we look for exemplary adults and young adults who live the values at the heart of America and engage them in programs designed to inspire and involve others.

Bill Halamandaris, the Foundation's president, serves as a full-time volunteer. A portion of the proceeds from this book will benefit each of the Heart of America Foundation's® four programs. These programs include:

The Ambassador Program, an educational outreach service for schools and youth groups that places exemplary young adults, like those profiled in this book, before as many of their peers as possible. Each ambassador speaks from personal experience, helping students understand their "response ability" and encouraging them to live up to their highest possibilities.

Heroes of the Heart™, a recognition program designed to identify and honor exemplary individuals who represent the heart of America.

Books from the Heart™, a literacy program which engages students, corporations and other organizations in gathering books that are not being used, solicits publishers for surplus books, and then gets these books to where they are needed most—the hands of children who have little to read and onto the empty shelves of impoverished school libraries.

Speaking from the Heart™, a professional nonprofit speakers program with a registry of more than 200 presenters, including many of those featured in this book.

If you would like to arrange an appearance by one of our speakers, contact one of the people featured in this book or find out more about their charities, write The Heart of America Foundation® at the address above or e-mail us at *HOACoreValues@aol.com.*

General information about The Heart of America Foundation® can be found on our website—
www.heartofamerica.org

Bibliography

Ben Carson:

Lewis, Gregg & Deborah Shaw, *Ben Carson.* Grand Rapids, Michigan: Zondervan, 2002.

Potter, Joan and Constance Claytor, *African Americans Who Were First.* New York: Cobblehill Books.

Tom Chappell:

Tom Chappell, *The Soul of Business: Managing for Profit and the Common Good.* New York: Bantam Press, 1993.

Caring People Magazine, Winter 1993, Washington, D.C., Caring Institute.

Mychal F. Judge:

Feister, John, "No Greater Love," *American Catholic,* October 2001.

"Remembering the Lost," *Newsday,* September 13, 2001.

"His Parish Knew No Bounds," *Los Angeles Times,* September 16, 2001.

Aaron Feuerstein:
Boulay, Art, "Malden Mills: A Study in Leadership," *Quality Monitor Newsletter,* October 1996.
Campbell, Kenneth D., MIT Tech Talk, April 16, 1972.
"The Mensch of Malden Mills," *CBS News,* July 6, 2003.
"Great Success Stories," *Forbes.*

David Morris:
Henderson, Nancy Bearden, "Doing the Right Thing," *Southwest Airlines Spirit,* May 2003.

Paul Newman:
NPR, "NPR Plays Ping-Pong with Paul Newman," *All Things Considered,* December 17, 1997.

Christopher Reeve:
CNN.COM, *Paula Zahn Now,* January 1, 2004.

Oprah Winfrey:
Oprah.com, 2004
Academy of Achievement, Hall of Business, 1989.
"Oprah Winfrey," *Time*, December 15, 2003.